Internal Control and Fraud Detection

Internal Control and Fraud Detection

Dr. Jae K. Shim, MBA, Ph.D.

Professor of Accounting and Finance
California State University, Long Beach
and
CEO, Delta Consulting Company

GLOBAL
professional
publishing

Global Professional Publishing Ltd
Random Acres
Slip Mill Lane
Hawkhurst
Cranbrook
Kent TN18 5AD
Email: publishing@gppbooks.com

Global Professional Publishing believes that the sources of information upon which the book is based are reliable, and has made every effort to ensure the complete accuracy of the text. However, neither Global Professional Publishing, the authors nor any contributors can accept any legal responsibility whatsoever for consequences that may arise from errors or omissions or any opinion or advice given.

ISBN 978-1-906403-62-1

Printed by Berforts, United Kingdom

For full details of Global Professional Publishing titles in Management, Finance and Banking see our website at:
www.gppbooks.com

Table of Contents

	Preface	vii
1	**Internal Control and the Internal Audit Function**	**1**
2	**Internal Audit of Financial Statement Accounts**	**25**
3	**Statististical Sampling in Tests of Controls**	**67**
4	**Fraud Prevention, Fraud Detection and Forensic Accounting**	**79**
	Appendix A: Indicators of Financial Crime	**127**
	Appendix B: Internal Control Forms and Checklists	**133**
	Glossary	**185**
	Index	**187**

Preface

Internal Control and Fraud Detection covers the essential tools you need to perform internal-control related services. It will take you, step by step, through your clients' responsibilities to design and implement programs and controls to prevent, deter, and detect fraud.

In doing so it touches on recent issues such as maintaining internal control over financial reporting in accordance with Section 404 of the Sarbanes-Oxley Act — "Enhanced Financial Disclosures, Management Assessment of Internal Control" — which mandates sweeping changes. Additionally Section 404, in conjunction with the related SEC rules and Auditing Standard (AS) No. 5 (An Audit of Internal Control Over Financial Reporting Performed in Conjunction with an Audit of Financial Statements), established by the Public Company Accounting Oversight Board (PCAOB), requires that the management of a public company and the company's independent auditor issue two new reports at the end of every fiscal year. These reports must then be included in the company's annual report filed with the Securities and Exchange Commission (SEC).

The book also covers Management's Antifraud Programs and Controls and the risk factors included in SAS No. 99. A major section then deals with forensic accounting, a specialty requiring the integration of investigative, accounting, and auditing skills. The forensic accountant looks at documents and financial and other data in a critical manner in order to draw conclusions, to calculate values, and to identify irregular patterns and/or suspicious transactions. As experts in this area, forensic accountants understand the fraud risk areas and have extensive fraud knowledge and experience of detecting and dealing with it. They do not merely look at the numbers but, rather, look critically behind the numbers in search of significant patterns.

Finally *Internal Control and Fraud Detection* provides its readers with practical guides and checklists such as indicators of financial crime, the ACFE's fraud prevention checkup, an internal control assessment form, computer applications checklist, and financial reporting information systems and controls checklist.

All in all this book will guide its readers to expertise in a specialist, but essential, area of managing their business.

Dr. Jae K. Shim

Dr. Jae K. Shim is one of the most prolific accounting and finance experts in the world. He is a professor of accounting and finance at California State University, Long Beach and CEO of Delta Consulting Company, a financial consulting and training firm. Dr. Shim received his M.B.A. and Ph.D. degrees from the University of California at Berkeley (Haas School of Business). He has been a consultant to commercial and nonprofit organizations for over 30 years.

Dr. Shim has over 50 college and professional books to his credit, including, *Barron's Accounting Handbook, Barron's Dictionary of Accounting Terms, 2011 GAAP: Handbook of Policies and Procedures, Budgeting Basics and Beyond, 2010-2011 Corporate Controller's Handbook of Financial Management, US Master Finance Guide, Uses and Analysis of Financial Statements, Investment Sourcebook, Dictionary of Real Estate, Dictionary of International Investment Terms, Dictionary of Business Terms, The Vest-Pocket CPA, The Vest-Pocket CFO,* and the best-selling *Vest-Pocket MBA.*

Thirty of his publications have been translated into foreign languages such as Chinese, Spanish, Russian, Polish, Croatian, Italian, Japanese, and Korean. Professor Shim's books have been published by CCH, Barron's, John Wiley, McGraw-Hill, Prentice-Hall, Penguins Portfolio, Thomson Reuters, Global Professional Publishing, American Management Association (Amacom), and the American Institute of CPAs (AICPA).

Dr. Shim has also published numerous articles in professional and academic journals. He was the recipient of the Financial Management Association International's *1982 Credit Research Foundation Award* for his article on cash flow forecasting and financial modeling.

Dr. Shim has been frequently quoted by such media as the *Los Angeles Times, Orange County Register, Business Start-ups, Personal Finance,* and *Money Radio.* He also provides business content He also provides business content for CPE e-learning providers and for m-learning providers such as iPhone, iPad, iPod, Blackberry, Android, Droid, and Nokia.

Email: drjaekshim@gmail.com, jaeshim@csulb.edu

Web: www.csulb.edu/~jaeshim

CHAPTER 1

Internal Control and the Internal Audit Function

Internal auditing serves as an independent appraisal activity within an entity for the review of accounting, financial, and other operations as a basis of service to management. Internal auditing can help improve the efficiency and profitability of the business. Proper review and appraisal of policies is essential. Audit procedures should be periodically performed on a cycle basis so that all individuals will know that the activity may be subject to audit. The primary purpose of audit procedures is to comply with United States generally accepted accounting principles (GAAP), not to detect errors or fraud.

The purposes of internal auditing are to:

▶ Understand the nature and scope of the activity/function.
▶ Check on the administrative efficiency in terms of current policies and procedures. At the same time, determine the extent of actual compliance with those policies and procedures.
▶ Appraise policies and procedures in terms of possible improvement.
▶ Increase efficiency (i.e., corporate welfare) by identifying any other means by which the activity/function can be made more effective.

▶ Ascertain the extent to which company assets are accounted for and safe-guarded from losses of all kinds.

▶ Determine the reliability of management data developed within the organization.

Also relevant is the efficiency with which the various units of the organization are conducting their assigned tasks. Specific audit tasks should be properly communicated to staff by means of formal written documents.

Problem areas have to be uncovered, especially vulnerable ones. For example, the internal auditor's examination of sales, receivables, and credit activities may point to poor credit policies or policies having a negative effect on profitability.

A vital aspect of internal auditing is the evaluation of internal control. Emphasis should be placed on the prevention rather than on the detection of fraud. The internal auditor should preferably be a planner, minimizing the conditions under which fraudulent activity may cultivate. If there is strong internal control, fraud has a higher probability of being detected. This chapter considers the internal control of the company, internal audit techniques and approaches, audit programs, and internal audit reports.

A company's internal control structure consists of management's policies and procedures which are designed to provide reasonable, but not absolute, assurance that specific entity objectives will be achieved.

Internal auditing aspects

Internal auditing deals with those procedures and techniques emphasizing adherence to management policies, existence of internal controls, uncovering fraud, existence of proper record keeping, and effective operations of the business. The major elements of the internal auditor's task are to determine the reliability and accuracy of accounting information, determine whether corporate data have been maintained in accordance with corporate policies and rules (e.g., manuals), and ascertain the adequacy of the internal control function. Internal auditing is the "eyes and ears of management." It deals not only with financial auditing but also operational auditing. Internal auditing should be carried out in conformity with the *Standards for the Professional Practice of Internal Auditing* and with the *Code of Ethics of The Institute of Internal Auditors (*www.theiia.org). *Note:* The Certified Internal Auditor (CIA) was created in 1974 by the Institute of Internal auditors (IIA). The CIA exam covers the four areas: internal audit process, internal audit skills, management control and information technology, and the audit environment.

Besides looking at the safeguarding and existence of assets, the internal auditor must be satisfied that resources are used economically and efficiently. Are actual results in conformity with objectives?

The internal auditor plans the scope of the audit, conducts the audit, appraises the operation, communicates results to the audit manager and auditee, and follows up to ensure that deficiencies have been recognized and outlines the steps that should be taken. The purpose of internal auditing is to ensure that there is proper discharge of responsibilities. The internal auditor provides analyses, appraisals, recommendations, and relevant comments regarding the activities.

Internal auditing involves many activities including:

▶ Reviewing and evaluating the reasonableness, adequacy, and application of accounting, financial, and other operating information and controls. Effective controls should be implemented at reasonable cost. For example, the telephone system should give a reading of numbers called, and should block out certain exchange calls (i.e., 900 calls).

▶ Determining the degree of compliance with policies.

▶ Ascertaining the degree to which corporate assets are accounted for and safeguarded.

▶ Evaluating the quality of performance in conducting responsibilities.

▶ Determining the reliability of management data.

▶ Recommending improvements in performance.

▶ Assisting in ways to improve profit performance.

▶ Conducting special audits such as developing new procedures as well as the acquisition of subsidiaries and divisions.

In the audit process:

▶ Determining the audit scope during preaudit through the review of management reports and risk analysis. For example, the audit objective might be to determine if purchase orders are authorized and processed in accordance with policy.

▶ Identify applicable criteria for evaluation to determine acceptance or nonacceptance. An appropriate standard will have to be developed, such as anything over 10% is considered excessive (depends on materiality and risk).

▶ Collect and evaluate information. An example is computing the actual turnover rate.

▶ Compare information against evaluative criteria. An example is comparing the actual turnover rate of 25% to a standard turnover rate of 10%.

▶ Form a conclusion, such as the turnover rate is excessive.

▶ Formulate and communicate recommendations to solve the problem at hand.

An audit tool is a means by which the internal auditor achieves his or her objective. It may be either manual or automated. An example of an audit tool is the use of questionnaires in assessing internal control. Common tools in internal auditing include internal control questionnaires, narratives, flowcharts, and audit software. These tools serve to develop an understanding of the area being audited. An auditor should prepare documentation of internal control during an audit. Examples of an auditor's documentation include flowcharts, narrative memoranda, questionnaires, and decision tables. A narrative memorandum is a written description of the process and flow of documents and of the control points.

The amount of audit evidence required depends on the conclusions to be reached from the preliminary survey and the sufficiency of internal control. The audit evidence typically relates to random pieces of information applying to particular events or transactions. Flowcharting is helpful in presenting a pictorial format.

The work papers should detail the transactions or accounts examined, the degree of testing, exceptions, and conclusions. The scope of the tests made should be described along with the details of any errors or deficiencies. A record of internal audit operations is especially important when the company does not have standardized procedures.

In a new assignment, the internal auditor will initially examine the organization chart to determine the "key" people involved. For example, in examining procurement, those responsible for purchasing, accounts payable, and treasury functions will be identified. Interviews with these individuals will be made to develop an understanding of the system.

The purpose of testing data for a specific application is to evaluate the appropriateness of current controls, determine compliance with present policies and procedures regarding data reliability, and substantiate processed transactions.

The extent of audit testing necessary depends upon the quality of internal control, the areas tested, and the particular circumstances. If controls seem appropriate, the internal auditor will test whether those controls are indeed operating effectively. If no reliance on the controls exists, the usual substantive testing will be extended.

In weak internal control situations, detailed verification is required. Here, a large sample is needed. Less field work is necessary when the company has significant self-checking devices to highlight defects and alert management to control breakdowns. Of course, the self-checking devices will still have to be scrutinized by the internal auditor.

In audit testing, the actual results of examining selected transactions or processes are compared to prescribed standards. In so doing, the internal auditor will be able to form an audit opinion. Some or all of the transactions, functions, activities, records, and statements are examined.

The following steps are usually involved in audit testing:

▶ determining standards
▶ defining the population
▶ selecting a sample, and
▶ examining the sampled items.

Standards

Standards may be explicit or implicit. Explicit standards are clearly stated in job instructions, directives, laws, and specifications. An example of an explicit standard is that competitive bids must be received on contracts in excess of $500,000. However, competitive bids may be "rigged" by specification requirements so that only certain suppliers can compete. Implicit standards exist when management formulates objectives and goals but does not establish in particular how they are to be accomplished. In this case, the internal auditor, upon completing a review of the objectives considering the controls in place, will consult with management regarding what is satisfactory performance.

In travel, the policy of upgrading from coach class should be spelled out. Is there a separate travel department? Are employees abusing the frequent flier privilege? There should be a written policy of who may be entertained and how much may be incurred. What is the policy regarding company vehicles? The personal use of office supplies, copiers, and fax machines must also be controlled.

In proportional analysis, the auditor evaluates certain revenue and expense items by relating them to other revenue and expenses. For instance, the cost of shipping cartons should have a proportional relationship to the number of units sold and shipped.

The population

The population to be tested takes into account audit objectives. If the purpose is to derive an opinion on transactions occurring after last year, all transactions constitute the population. If the objective is to formulate an opinion regarding current controls, the population becomes more restricted. Management wants to know if the system is working properly. If not, ways to improve it must be formulated.

In deriving the population to be tested, a determination must be made of the total transactions (e.g., purchase orders, invoices, billings). These should be serially numbered. If documents are missing, the reasons must be uncovered. The character and location of the inventory must be determined. Are transactions stratified by value or other characteristic?

Whether verifications and analyses are carried out in detail or on a test check basis depends on the importance of the item and the likelihood of material misstatement. In test-checking, a statistical sample is selected.

The sample

The sample should be selected according to the audit objective, whether it be judgmental or statistical. Reliable selection is from lists that are separate from the records themselves. This assures that items which may have been removed from the physical units have not been overlooked.

Statistical sampling used in the internal auditing process include random, discovery, and multistage. Sampling techniques are used to verify such things as recorded amounts in the financial statements and product quality control.

The internal auditor should be assured that there is proper communication within the organization. Needed information should be available when a decision must be made and it must go to the appropriate party. The information must be clearly understood.

To develop an understanding of internal control, the internal auditor must become familiar with the operating unit or area being audited, including knowledge about the design of relevant controls and whether they have been placed in operation. Reviewing the entity's descriptions of inventory policies and procedures helps the auditor understand their design. The stages in this process are

- ▶ preaudit
- ▶ scope
- ▶ comprehending the structure
- ▶ verification, and
- ▶ evaluation.

Preaudit

Information is gathered and the internal auditor becomes thoroughly familiar with the factual content. Departments or operational sections should be separated in the work papers and cross-referenced where there are overlapping data.

Scope

The internal auditor meets with the unit or department manager to start the operational review in his or her area. The scope and objectives should be explained. The information should be filtered down through the organization. The internal auditor should stress that the purpose of an audit is to review internal controls and assess current operations to provide recommendations to improve controls and maximize efficiency to attain the company goal of maximizing profits. A meeting with the manager and supervisory personnel may be in order, depending on the size, and the like. The following should be reviewed with the manager: organization charts, departmental budgets, policy manuals, procedure manuals, flowcharts, activities listings, forms and reports, records, and questions developed in the preaudit.

Comprehending Internal Control

Based upon the information furnished by the department manager and other key employees, the internal auditor completes the applicable departmental internal control questionnaire (e.g., purchasing questionnaire). A general summary of the internal auditor's view of the existing situation and activities should be prepared for the functional unit under review. Questionnaires are reviewed and a determination is made of who is to be interviewed. Sample internal control questionnaires are provided later in the chapter. Questions should be summarized before interviewing to assure a planned approach and to minimize interview time and maximize efficiency of the audit. You should show a desire to understand the person's job, its importance, and difficult tasks. You should review in detail the questionnaires and discuss matters requiring clarification. In the course of interviewing, a definite effort should be made to put the employee at ease and draw out his or her complaints, criticisms, and improvement suggestions relative to the employee's individual job, the department's operations, and divisional operations. You should summarize the results of the interview, paying particular attention to criticisms, complaints, and constructive suggestions to improve operations.

It is then appropriate to determine specific areas to carry over into the evaluation phase, which may require the preparation of specific worksheets for further clarification. Some worksheets that may be required are: departmental functional activity analysis, forms involved in job function, reports generated or received by department, process worksheets, and paperwork flow analysis.

Verification

During each segment of the verification phase, every situation uncovered and summarized in the scope and understanding phases of this review must be kept in mind. Refer to the summaries throughout this phase, testing each situation to your own satisfaction. Challenge every aspect of significant situations to reveal every opportunity for possible improvement.

Each area requires different techniques and amounts of verification. These will be dictated by the outcome of the scope and understanding phases. Based on departmental files and volume or population information, determine specific documents to be selected for sampling and prepare a listing of such documents to be accumulated by divisional personnel, if possible (selection of sample items), since the audit is limited to a specified time frame. Upon receipt of documents requested for sampling, enter required information and any other pertinent remarks on the sampling worksheet. While performing this step, determine compliance with policies and procedures, effectiveness of internal control, and possible areas for improvement. Before proceeding with this step, reference should be made to specific program segments for the department involved. Where a specific report indicates a need for improvement in internal control, operation efficiency and so on, the specific items in question should be checked and followed up with the responsible operating personnel. Notes should be prepared, summarizing the results of the follow-up with each employee contacted. Time devoted to this effort should be charged to this audit segment regardless of the specific segment in which the point in question arose.

Evaluation

When the first four phases have been completed in each area, final evaluation should be initiated. Because of the understanding gained during the course of the review, it is extremely difficult not to form hasty opinions and initiate some preliminary evaluation throughout the review. This should be avoided. The final evaluation is the basis upon which you will determine recommendations and prepare the report, with all the facts being considered in their proper perspective. From the various data, interview notes, and verification summaries, prepare a summary of the major areas of improvement opportunity.

Work out details of report points and recommendations. Review these with other members of the audit team and appropriate divisional personnel. Restudy and verify apparent conflicts of facts or uncertain points. After this review and verification, finalize the report points and review again with other members of the audit team. When report points are finalized and there is agreement on the recommendations, set up a closing meeting with supervisors to coincide with reviews in other areas. Review report points and recommendations with local management.

Internal audit reports

The internal audit report should explain the scope of the review and detailed audit findings. In the report, there should be a statement of the general scope of the examination. Further, background information should be given. If limiting factors exist, they should be stated. The body of the audit report contains details of the examination, which is cross-referenced to the summary. Written reports may emphasize:

▶ Details of verification including reasons for and disposition of exceptions.

▶ Financial accounting data.
▶ Information of special executive interest, such as highlighting unusual or defective situations along with corrective action, which will be taken by the auditee.

The internal audit report should include a summary of major findings and recommendations. A conclusion about what was uncovered by the audit will be provided. The internal audit report must be factual, based on hard evidence.

In forming the internal audit opinion, the auditor will typically express opinions on the findings. Contrary opinions by operating management should be noted. Even though opinions may differ, a disagreement as to facts should not exist. The internal auditor's conclusion should be stated clearly with objective support.

To nonaccountants, narrative reports are more meaningful than numerical tabulations. If there is significant numerical information, this should be contained in an exhibit supplementing the report. The body of the report should have a summary of the relevant reference to the exhibit and its importance.

All internal audit reports should contain the same basic structure, including:

▶ *Identification.* The name of the report should identify the unit or operational area reviewed. The auditors involved in the examination should be named. Give the date of the report along with the test period. Determine if the report is a regular one or a follow-up. Indicate the name of the auditor issuing the report.

▶ *Summary.* Highlight the major points for management so that it is easier to identify areas requiring action.

▶ *Scope.* Describe the objectives of the audit work performed.

▶ *Background.* Provide relevant background information to understand the findings and recommendations of the audit report. Examples are sales volume and number of employees.

▶ *Findings.* Present findings relating to the factual information uncovered in the review. The audit findings should be given in logical order of importance, or in terms of functions, phases, or account classifications. Prior to report issuance, findings should be discussed with local (auditee) management in a closing meeting to minimize disputes. If the dispute is unresolved, the positions of the auditor and management should be given. Where corrective action has been implemented by management it should be referred to in the report.

▶ *Opinion and recommendations.* Present conclusions regarding the findings. Propose suggestions to solve the problems.

▶ *Signature.* Have the auditor-in-charge sign the report.

▶ *Acknowledgement.* Provide a statement recognizing help given the auditor by the manager along with a request for a reply to the report.

▶ *Appendices* (optional). Appendices should contain information not needed to comprehend the report but valuable if detailed information is desired. Examples are a listing of standards violated, explanations, and statistical information. These data should be after the body of the report.

▶ *Graphics* (optional). Graphics help explain material in the report including graphs, charts, pictorial representations, and photographs. For instance, a flowchart can explain how a recommendation may be implemented.

The format of the internal audit report depends on the kind of report being issued (e.g., formal versus informal), the readers being addressed, and nature and reasoning of the auditing activity. Different auditing organizations will use different report formats and divide their reports into different subsections. The format should be consistently used. The internal audit report must be accurate, concise, clear, and timely. The internal audit report should be distributed to those who have authority to take corrective action.

Audit program

In planning, the auditor should consider the nature, timing, and extent of work to be performed and should prepare a written audit program. An audit program sets forth in reasonable detail the audit procedures necessary to accomplish audit objectives. The audit program should be tailored to the specific internal audit assignment. Each work step should indicate why the procedure is being performed, the objective, and controls being tested. In-depth analysis and evaluations are required. There should be flexibility in the audit program so that a prescribed procedure may be altered or work extended depending on particular circumstances. Unusual risks should be identified and controls needed to eliminate that risk should be recommended. Audit findings should be stated along with recommended corrective action.

Compliance auditing

An essential part of internal auditing is substantiating compliance with company and regulatory policies, procedures, and laws. It is essential to review whether employees are conducting their tasks as desired by management. Assurance must be obtained that controls are functioning and responsible parties have been assigned. There should be written compliance directives in such sources as manuals, bulletins, and letters.

In compliance testing, the internal auditor examines evidence to substantiate that the firm's internal control structure elements are performing as intended.

Note: It is best to verify that internal controls are working through testing practices of the operations of the control techniques themselves instead of verifying the results of processing.

A key aspect of internal auditing deals with compliance as to accounting procedures. The accounting system must be operating as designed if reliable and consistent accounting data are to be provided. The appropriate forms have to be used in the prescribed manner.

Examples of areas subject to compliance testing are standards for data processing, controller's procedures, procurement, data retention requirements of the company and governmental agencies, security policies, personnel administration, planning, budgeting, payroll, and expense accounts.

Operational auditing

Operational auditing looks at the effectiveness, efficiency, and economy of operational performance in the business. It examines the reasonableness of recorded financial information. The performance of managers and staff are scrutinized. For example, there should be an examination of operational performance related to payroll, receiving, purchasing, and cost control. Generally, operations should be conducted in such a way that results in profitability.

A determination must be made as to whether corporate policies are being adhered to as well as whether such policies are reasonable in the current environment or if changes are necessary. Areas of inefficiency and uneconomical practice are identified.

Some internal audit departments have engineers to appraise productivity and assist in formulating work standards. Operational performance criteria include the sufficiency of resources acquired, response time to requests, efficient utilization of personnel, proper supervision, up-to-date equipment and technology, and adequacy of storage.

Management auditing

The management audit is a special type of operational audit. Its ultimate outcome is the same, namely to achieve operating effectiveness and efficiency. But the more immediate concern of the management auditor is more on the effectiveness of the management function than on efficiency. Management audits involve and affect management, typically all the way up to the senior level.

Functional auditing

A functional audit looks at a process from beginning to end, crossing organizational lines. Functional auditing emphasizes operations and processes rather than administration and people. It looks at how well each department handles the function involved. Are departments cooperating in carrying out the task effectively and efficiently? Examples of functional audits relate to safety practices, uncovering conflicts of interest, changing products, ordering and paying for materials, and deliveries of supplies to user departments.

In performing a functional audit, auditors have to define job parameters, keep the parameters within reasonable range, and cover all major aspects of the function. Functional audits deal with several organizations, some where conflicts of interest exist. The advantages of functional audits are obtaining diverse viewpoints, identifying problem areas, reconciling different objectives, and highlighting duplications.

The internal auditor may be asked to engage in a special review of ongoing programs. A program relates to any funded effort for typical ongoing activities of the company. Examples include an employee benefit program, a new contract, an expansion program, a new computerized application, and a training program. The internal auditor provides management with cost data and the results of the program. Possible alternative ways of carrying out the function at less cost are examined.

Financial auditing

In financial auditing, there is a determination of whether the financial statements present fairly the financial position and operating results of a company in accordance with generally accepted accounting principles. The company must comply with the relevant organizational policies and procedures as well as the laws and regulations governing the business. Work performed in an internal financial audit can be used to reduce fees of the external auditor.

Appraising internal control

An entity's internal control consists of five interrelated components:
- Control environment.
- Risk assessment.
- Control activities.
- Information and communication.
- Monitoring.

The control environment

The control environment sets the tone of an organization. It includes human resource policies and practices relative to hiring, orientation, training, evaluating, counseling, promoting, compensating, and remedial actions. The control environment, which is the foundation for the other components of internal control, provides discipline and structure by setting the tone of an organization and influencing control consciousness.

The factors to consider in assessing the control environment include:

▶ Integrity and ethical values, including: (1) management's actions to eliminate or mitigate incentives and temptations on the part of personnel to commit dishonest, illegal, or unethical acts; (2) policy statements; and (3) codes of conduct.

▶ Commitment to competence, including management's consideration of competence levels for specific tasks and how those levels translate into necessary skills and knowledge.

▶ Board of directors or audit committee participation, including interaction with internal and external (independent) auditors.

▶ Management's philosophy and operating style, such as management's attitude and actions regarding financial reporting, as well as management's approach to taking and monitoring risks.

▶ The entity's organizational structure (i.e., the form and nature of organizational units).

▶ Assignment of authority and responsibility, including fulfilling job responsibilities.

▶ Human resource policies and practices, including those relating to hiring, orientation, training, evaluating, counseling, promoting, and compensating employees.

In obtaining an understanding of the control environment, the auditor seeks to understand the attitude, awareness, and actions concerning the control environment on the part of management and the directors. For this purpose, the auditor must concentrate on the substance of controls rather than their form because controls may be established but not acted upon. For example, management may adopt a code of ethics but condone violations of the code.

Risk assessment

An auditor should assess the risk that errors and fraud may cause the financial statements to contain material misstatements. (S)he should then design the audit so as to provide reasonable assurance that material errors and fraud are detected. An entity's risk assessment for financial reporting purposes is its identification, analysis, and management of risks pertaining to financial statement preparation. Accordingly, risk assessment may consider the possibility of executed transactions that remain unrecorded.

The following internal and external events and circumstances may be relevant to the risk of preparing financial statements that are not in conformity with United

States generally accepted accounting principles (or another comprehensive basis of accounting):

▶ Changes in operating and regulatory environment, including competitive pressures.

▶ New personnel that have a different perspective on internal control.

▶ Rapid growth that can result in a breakdown in controls.

▶ New technology in information systems and production processes.

▶ New lines, products, or activities.

▶ Corporate restructuring that might result in changes in supervision and segregation of job functions.

▶ Expanded foreign operations.

▶ Accounting pronouncements requiring adoption of new accounting principles.

Control activities

Control activities are the policies and procedures management has implemented in order to ensure that directives are carried out. Control activities may be classified into the following categories:

▶ *Performance reviews*, including comparisons of actual performance with budgets, forecasts, and prior-period results.

▶ *Information processing*. Controls relating to information processing are generally designed to verify accuracy, completeness, and authorization of transactions. Specifically, controls may be classified as general controls or application controls. The former might include controls over data center operations, systems software acquisition and maintenance, and access security; the latter apply to the processing of individual applications and are designed to ensure that transactions that are recorded are valid, authorized, and complete.

▶ *Physical controls*, which involve adequate safeguards over the access to assets and records, include authorization for access to computer programs and files and periodic counting and comparison with amounts shown on control records.

▶ *Segregation of duties*, which is designed to reduce the opportunities to allow any person to be in a position both to perpetrate and to conceal errors or irregularities (fraud) in the normal course of his or her duties, involves assigning different people the responsibilities of authorizing transactions, recording transactions, and maintaining custody of assets.

Information and communication systems support

The information system generally consists of the methods and records established to record, process, summarize, and report entity transactions and to maintain accountability of related assets, liabilities, and equity.

Communication involves providing an understanding of individual roles and responsibilities pertaining to internal control.

Monitoring

Monitoring is management's process of assessing the quality of internal control performance over time. Accordingly, management must assess the design and operation of controls on a timely basis and take necessary corrective actions.

Monitoring may involve: (1) separate evaluations, (2) the use of internal auditors, and (3) the use of communications from outside parties (e.g., complaints from customers and regulator comments).

The role of the internal audit function

An auditor's primary concern is whether a specific control affects financial statement assertions. Much of the audit work required to form an opinion consists of gathering evidence about the assertions in the financial statements. These assertions are management representations embodied in the components of the financial statements. Controls relevant to an audit are individually or in combination likely to prevent or detect material misstatements in financial statement assertions.

The internal audit function should play an important role in the monitoring of internal control. The internal auditor must obtain a sufficient knowledge of the five interrelated components in order to: (1) identify the types of misstatements that could occur in the financial records and (2) ensure that the entity operates in such a way that goals are efficiently and effectively met. Since the entity's external auditors will most likely attempt to utilize internal control to restrict their testing of financial statement assertions, it is important that internal control be properly established and maintained.

The cycle approach

In setting up effective internal control, management should utilize the cycle approach, which first stratifies internal control into broad areas of activity and then identifies specific classes of transactions. Accordingly, the following cycles should be considered:

▶ *Revenue Cycle*: revenue and accounts receivable (order processing, credit approval, shipping, invoicing, and recording) and cash receipts.

▶ *Expenditure Cycle*: purchasing, receiving, accounts payable, payroll, and cash disbursements.

▶ *Production or Conversion Cycle*: inventories; cost of sales; and property, plant, and equipment.

▶ *Financing Cycle*: notes receivable and investments, notes payable, debt, leases, other obligations, and equity accounts.

▶ *External Reporting*: accounting principles and preparation of financial statements.

Identifying deficiencies in internal control and fraud

Internal control should be monitored in order to identify deficiencies which could adversely affect: (1) the operation of the entity, and (2) the financial statement presentation. The internal audit function has the responsibility of testing compliance with the policies and procedures (i.e., controls) embodied in internal control. Internal control can provide reasonable assurance that certain management objectives implicit in internal control are achieved. Internal control can also provide reasonable assurance that transactions are recorded as necessary to permit preparation of financial statements in conformity with United States GAAP or any other applicable criteria and to maintain accountability for assets. Because of inherent limitations, however, internal control cannot be designed to eliminate all fraud.

The illustrative internal control forms presented in Figures 1, 2, and 3 in the Appendix should prove useful in monitoring internal control. Although normally utilized by an outside independent auditor, the forms are also appropriate for internal use since management objectives are clearly addressed.

The internal auditor must always be aware of the possibility of fraud. Fraud involves the taking of something of value from someone else through deceit. Fraud may involve the following:

▶ Failing to record sales while simultaneously stealing cash receipts

▶ Creating overages in cash funds and cash registers by intentionally under-recording cash receipts.

▶ The issuance of credit for counterfeit customer claims and returns

▶ Recording unwarranted cash discounts.

▶ Increasing amounts of suppliers' invoices by means of collusion.

▶ Overstating sales to obtain bonuses.

Possible indicators of management fraud include:

▶ Lack of compliance with company directives and procedures.

▶ Payments made to trade creditors which are supported by copies instead of original invoices.

▶ Consistently late reports.

▶ Higher commissions which are not based on increased sales.

▶ Managers who habitually assume the duties of their subordinates.

▶ Managers who handle matters not within the scope of their authority.

The internal auditor must also be cognizant of embezzlement schemes. Possible indicators of embezzlement include:

▶ The tendency to cover up inefficiencies or "plug" figures.

▶ Excessive criticism of others in order to divert suspicion.

▶ Displaying annoyance with reasonable questioning.

▶ The continued willingness to work overtime.

▶ Reluctance to give custody of assets to others.

▶ The providing of misinformation or vague answers.

Internal control taken as a whole should therefore provide a system of checks and balances. As a result, no one individual should have complete control over a transaction from beginning to end. Furthermore, periodic rotation of job functions is essential. A proper system of internal checks and balances makes it difficult for an employee to steal cash or other assets and concurrently cover up the misappropriation by entering corresponding amounts in the accounts.

Key documents (for example, sales invoices) should be prenumbered and used in sequential order. Additionally, custody of and access to these documents should be controlled.

All parties involved in a particular transaction or activity should receive copies of the documents involved (example: invoice, order, correspondence). This provides an audit trail and aids in coordination among interested parties and assists in detecting errors and irregularities. Accordingly, good internal control requires standard policies regarding the distribution of materials throughout the organization. Access to inventory should be restricted.

Employee responsibilities should be monitored as far down in the company as practical. Employees will act more responsibly if they know that they are accountable and will have to justify deviations from prescribed procedures.

Transactions should be executed only after appropriate authorization is obtained. There are two types of authorization to be considered. General authorization specifies definite limits on what an employee can do without intervention of management, for example, prices to charge, discounts which may be offered, and what costs are reimbursable. Specific authorization typically means that supervisory personnel must approve in writing a specific deviation from a company policy. For example, written authorization may be required for corporate expense reimbursement above a prescribed limit.

The Foreign Corrupt Practices Act

According to the Foreign Corrupt Practices Act of 1977 (FCPA), SEC-reporting companies must maintain books, records, and accounts that accurately reflect transactions. In this regard, the company must establish and maintain effective internal control that provides reasonable assurance that:

▶ Recorded transactions permit the preparation of financial statements in conformity with generally accepted accounting principles.

▶ Accountability over assets exists.

▶ Transactions are entered into in conformity with management's general or specific authorization.

▶ Access to assets is only in accordance with corporate policies.

In addition, there should be periodic reconciliation of assets per books and the physical existence of such assets.

Internal auditors typically have the responsibility to see that the company's internal control is in conformity with the Foreign Corrupt Practices Act. The requirements of the FCPA relating to the maintenance of accounting records and systems of internal accounting control apply only to companies required to register under the Securities Exchange Act of 1934, The FCPA also contains prohibitions against bribery and other corrupt practices. The antibribery provisions apply to all domestic business concerns engaged in interstate commerce.

The Sarbanes-Oxley Act

Section 404 of the Sarbanes-Oxley Act — "Enhanced Financial Disclosures, Management Assessment of Internal Control" — mandates sweeping changes. Section 404, in conjunction with the related SEC rules and Auditing Standard (AS) No. 5, *An Audit of Internal Control Over Financial Reporting Performed in Conjunction with an Audit of Financial Statements)*, established by the Public Company Accounting Oversight Board (PCAOB), requires management of a public company and the company's independent auditor to issue two new reports at the end of every fiscal year. These reports must be included in the company's annual report filed with the Securities and Exchange Commission (SEC).

▶ *Management must report annually on the effectiveness of the company's internal control over financial reporting.*

▶ *In conjunction with the audit of the company's financial statements, the company's independent auditor must issue a report on internal control over financial reporting, which includes both an opinion on management's assessment and an opinion on the effectiveness of the company's internal control over financial reporting.*

In the past, a company's internal controls were considered in the context of planning the audit but were not required to be reported publicly, except in response to the SEC's Form 8-K requirements when related to a change in auditor. The new audit and reporting requirements have drastically changed the situation and have brought the concept of internal control over financial reporting to the forefront for audit committees, management, auditors, and users of financial statements.

The Auditing Standard No. 5 highlight the concept of a *significant* deficiency in internal control over financial reporting, and mandate that both management and the independent auditor must publicly report any material weaknesses in internal control over financial reporting that exist as of the fiscal year-end assessment date. A significant deficiency is a deficiency (i.e., control deficiency), or a combination of deficiencies, that is less severe than a material weakness yet important enough to merit attention by those having financial reporting oversight responsibility.

The main features of the AS No. 5 are summarized later in the chapter

1. What is internal control over financial reporting?

Internal control over financial reporting is a PROCESS designed and maintained by management to provide reasonable assurance regarding the reliability of financial reporting and the preparation of the financial statements for external purposes in accordance with United States generally accepted accounting principles (GAAP). It encompasses the processes and procedures management has established to:

▶ *Maintain records that accurately reflect the company's transactions*
▶ *Prepare financial statements and footnote disclosures for external purposes and provide reasonable assurance that receipts and expenditures are appropriately authorized*
▶ *Prevent or promptly detect unauthorized acquisition, use, or disposition of the company's assets that could have a material effect on the financial statements*

Internal control over financial reporting is defined more narrowly than the general term "internal control," which includes controls associated with the effectiveness and efficiency of operations and compliance with laws and regulations that are not directly related to the financial statements. For example, controls to improve safety or streamline manufacturing processes are not considered part of internal control over financial reporting.

An effective internal control structure involves people at all levels of the organization. It includes those who maintain accounting records, prepare and disseminate policies, monitor systems, and function in a variety of operating roles. In addition, a company's internal control over financial reporting is influenced significantly by its board of directors and the audit committee, which has ultimate responsibility for oversight of the financial reporting process.

The concept of reasonable assurance is integral to the definition of internal control over financial reporting and to management's assessment and the independent auditor's opinions. Reasonable assurance refers to the fact that internal controls — even when they are appropriately designed and operating effectively — cannot provide absolute assurance of achieving control objectives. Inherent limitations include the potential for human error or circumvention of controls. Reasonable assurance is a high level of assurance, but it is not absolute — it recognizes that even with an effective system of internal control over financial reporting, there is a possibility that material misstatements, including misstatements due to management fraud, may occur and not be prevented or detected on a timely basis.

It should be noted that the role of internal control over financial reporting is to support the integrity and reliability of the company's external financial reporting processes. It is not intended to provide any assurances about the company's operating performance, its future results, or the quality of its business model.

2. What are the responsibilities of management and the independent auditor with respect to internal control over financial reporting?

Management's role. Management is responsible for designing and implementing the system of internal control over financial reporting, for evaluating the effectiveness of internal control over financial reporting, and for issuing a public report on that assessment. Management is to base its assessment on a suitable, recognized control framework, such as that established by the Committee of Sponsoring Organizations of the Treadway Commission (COSO) and support its evaluation with sufficient documented evidence.

Auditor's role. Before the Sarbanes-Oxley Act was passed, the auditor was required to obtain an understanding of internal control sufficient to plan the audit of the financial statements. If material weaknesses were identified, they ordinarily were reported only to management and the audit committee. Section 404 now requires the auditor to perform an independent audit of internal control over financial reporting and to issue a report including two opinions — one on management's assessment and one on the effectiveness of internal control over financial reporting.

3. What is an auditor's objective in auditing internal control over financial reporting and what is meant by an integrating the audit of financial statements with the audit of internal control over financial reporting?

The objective of an audit of internal control over financial reporting is to express an opinion on the effectiveness of a company's internal control over financial reporting.

In an "integrated" audit, an auditor needs to design tests of controls to accomplish the objectives of both types of audits simultaneously. Accordingly, tests of controls should enable an auditor to obtain sufficient evidence to support (1) an opinion on the effectiveness of internal control over financial reporting and (2) the assessments of control risk for the audit of financial statements.

4. How will the new reporting model differ from historical reporting?

In the past, the independent auditor provided an opinion on whether the company's financial statements were presented fairly in all material respects, in accordance with United States GAAP. The new reporting model maintains this historical requirement for the auditor to express an opinion on the financial statements. Section 404 also institutes additional requirements for management and the independent auditor to report on the effectiveness of internal control over financial reporting, as shown in Table 1.

Table 1: Historical reporting versus new reporting

Historical reporting

Independent auditor's opinion on whether the financial statements are presented fairly in all material respects, in accordance with United States GAAP

New reporting

Management's report on its assessment of the effectiveness of the company's internal control over financial reporting

Independent auditor's report on internal control over financial reporting, including the auditor's opinions on: (1) whether management's assessment is fairly stated in all material respects (i.e., whether the auditor concurs with management's conclusions about the effectiveness of internal control, over financial reporting), and (2) the effectiveness of the company's internal control over financial reporting

The independent auditor's opinions on the financial statements and on internal control over financial reporting may be issued in a combined report or in separate reports. Table 2 identifies the various reports, and reflects the fact that management's assessment of internal control over financial reporting constitutes the starting point for the auditor's reporting.

Table 2: Section 404 reporting

```
                    ┌─────────────────────┐      ┌──────────────────────────┐
                    │       NOTE:          │      │     Management's         │
                    │  Auditor's reports   │      │  Section 404 Assessment  │
                    │   may be combined    │      │                          │
                    └─────────────────────┘      └──────────────────────────┘
                                                              │
                                                              │
  ┌──────────────────────┐                      ┌──────────────────────────┐
  │   Auditor's Report    │                     │    Auditor's Report on    │
  │  on the Audit of the  │◄────────────────────│       the Audit of        │
  │  Financial Statements │                     │   Internal Control over   │
  │                       │                     │   Financial Reporting     │
  └──────────────────────┘                      └──────────────────────────┘
            │                            ┌──────────────┴───────────┐
  ┌──────────────────────┐      ┌────────────────┐      ┌────────────────┐
  │   Opinion on the      │      │   Opinion on   │      │   Opinion on   │
  │ Financial Statements  │      │  Management's  │      │ Effectiveness  │
  │                       │      │  Assessments   │      │                │
  └──────────────────────┘      └────────────────┘      └────────────────┘
```

5. What will management's report include?

Neither the SEC nor the PCAOB has issued a standard or illustrative management report on internal control over financial reporting; thus, there may be differences in the nature and extent of the information companies provide. We advise companies to consult with legal counsel on these matters. At a minimum, management's report on internal control over financial reporting should include the following information:

- ▶ *Statement of management's responsibility for establishing and maintaining adequate internal control over financial reporting.*
- ▶ *Statement identifying the framework used by management to evaluate the effectiveness of internal control over financial reporting.*
- ▶ *Management's assessment of the effectiveness of the company's internal control over financial reporting as of the end of the company's most recent fiscal year, including an explicit statement as to whether that internal control is effective and disclosing any material weaknesses identified by management in that control.*
- ▶ *Statement that the registered public accounting firm that audited the financial statements included in the annual report has issued an attestation report on management's internal control assessment.*

Management's report must indicate that internal control over financial reporting is either:

- ▶ *Effective* - *Internal control over financial reporting is effective (i.e., no material weaknesses in internal control over financial reporting existed as of the assessment date); or*

▶ **Ineffective** — *Internal control is not effective because one or more material weaknesses existed as of management's assessment date.*

Management is required to state *whether or not* the company's internal control over financial reporting is effective. A negative assurance statement, such as "nothing has come to management's attention to suggest internal control is ineffective" is not acceptable.

If a material weakness exists as of the assessment date, management is required to conclude that internal control over financial reporting is not effective and to disclose all material weaknesses that may have been identified. The SEC Chief Accountant has stated publicly that he expects management's report to disclose the nature of any material weakness in sufficient detail to enable investors and other financial statement users to understand the weakness and evaluate the circumstances underlying it.

Management may not express a qualified conclusion, such as stating that internal control is effective except to the extent certain problems have been identified. If management is unable to assess certain aspects of internal control that are material to overall control effectiveness, management must conclude that internal control over financial reporting is ineffective. Although management cannot issue a report with a scope limitation, under specific conditions newly acquired businesses or certain other consolidated entities may be excluded from the assessment.

Key points of Auditing Standard No. 5

1. Focus the audit of internal control over financial reporting on the most important matters

AS5 articulates a key principle that a direct relationship exists between the risk of material weakness and the amount of auditor attention given to that area. It requires auditors to use a top-down, risk-based approach, beginning with the financial statements and company-level controls, and requires the auditor to perform a walk-through for each significant process before selecting the controls to test. Using this assessment, the auditor selects the controls to test based on the risk of a material weakness. AS5 emphasizes the integration of the financial statement audit with the audit of internal control over financial reporting.

2. Provide explicit and practical guidance on scaling the audit to fit the size and complexity of the company

These provisions do not create a separate standard for smaller companies. Instead, AS5 explicitly requires the auditor to tailor the nature, extent and timing of testing to meet the unique characteristics of smaller companies.

3. Eliminate procedures that are unnecessary to achieve the intended benefits

AS5 links the testing of specific controls to a risk assessment of that control. This means that the risk of a specific control not being effective should drive the nature, extent and timing of testing performed and evidence of effectiveness obtained for that control.

4. Require auditors to consider whether and how to use the work of others

AS5 allows auditors to place greater reliance on testing completed by management and the internal audit function. The scope of the new Auditing Standard applies to both the audit of internal control over financial reporting as well as the audit of financial statements -- eliminating a barrier to the integrated audit.

4. Incorporate guidance on efficiency

Many of the audit efficiency practices outlined in its May 16, 2005, guidance are contained in the new Standard. AS5 specifically includes the language from the May 16 guidance regarding the baselining of IT controls. As a result, companies can leverage this guidance to reduce compliance costs on a year-over-year basis.

5 A simplified standard

AS5 changes the definitions of material weakness from "more than remote" to "reasonably possible" and significant deficiency from "more than inconsequential" to "significant." AS5 defines "significant" as "less than material but merits the attention of those with the responsibility for the oversight of financial reporting." In other words, significant deficiencies are not material weaknesses but items that those responsible for oversight need to know about

CHAPTER 2

Internal Audit of Financial Statement Accounts

An important function of the internal audit staff is to ensure that the financial statements prepared by management are presented fairly, in all material respects, in conformity with generally accepted accounting principles. This will facilitate the annual audit performed by the independent certified public accountant. However, internal audit should coordinate with the independent auditors to avoid duplication of effort and to ensure risks of the company are adequately monitored.

This chapter addresses the objectives and procedures to consider in auditing major financial statement accounts. It is obvious that the results of audit testing should be clearly documented. Discrepancies between the audit results and the books and records should clearly be investigated. The exceptions could be indicative of widespread problems that could have an overall adverse effect on the entity.

Financial statements, in general, consist of assertions that are representations of the management of the company.

Specific financial statement assertions include:

- *Existence or occurrence* Assertions about existence or occurrence are concerned with whether assets or liabilities of the entity exist at a particular date and whether recorded transactions have truly occurred during a specified time period.
- *Completeness* Assertions pertaining to completeness apply to whether all transactions and accounts that should be included in the financial statements are actually included.

▶ *Rights and obligations* Assertions relating to rights and obligations deal with whether the entity has legal title to assets and whether the recorded liabilities are in fact obligations of the entity.

▶ *Valuation or allocation* Assertions about valuation or allocation are concerned with whether asset, liability, revenue, and expense components have been included in the financial statements at appropriate amounts.

▶ *Presentation and disclosure* Assertions about presentation and disclosure deal with whether particular components of the financial statements are properly described, disclosed, and classified.

After financial statement assertions are identified, the internal auditor should then develop audit objectives, which are often restatements of the broad assertions but fine tuned for the specific accounts being examined.

In developing an internal audit work program, the auditor must also establish the procedures to be used.

Some of the more common auditing procedures include:

▶ *Inquiry,* often defined as the seeking of information, is based on interviewing appropriate personnel at all organizational levels. The responses derived from inquiry may be written or oral but should be corroborated by more additional evidence.

▶ *Observation* involves watching employees perform their assigned functions.

▶ *Inspection* entails careful examination of pertinent documents and records as well as the physical examination of assets.

▶ *Tracing* involves tracking source documents from their creation to the recorded amounts in the books of original entry.

▶ *Reperformance* means repeating an activity.

▶ *Vouching* involves selecting amounts recorded in the books and examining documents that support those recorded amounts.

▶ *Scrutinizing* is a careful visual review of records, reports, and schedules in order to identify unusual items.

▶ *Confirmation* is a process whereby the auditor can obtain corroborating evidential matter from an independent party which is outside the organization.

▶ *Analytical procedures* involve the study and comparison of the plausible relationships that exist among financial and nonfinancial data. Analytical procedures include ratio analysis and comparisons of current-period financial information to: (1) prior-period financial information, (2) anticipated results, (3) predictable patterns, (4) similar information within the same industry, and (5) nonfinancial data. A basic premise underlying the application of analytical procedures is that plausible relationships among data may reasonably be expected to exist and continue in the absence of known conditions to the contrary. Variability in these relationships can be explained by, for example, unusual events or transactions, business or accounting changes, misstatements, or random fluctuations.

It should be understood that in addition to the procedures reviewed above, there are other basic procedures which may be used. Accordingly, the following should also be considered:

- ▶ Reading and reviewing pertinent documents.
- ▶ Analyzing details of account balances.
- ▶ Verifying the validity of statements or representations.

Since an audit procedure may enable satisfaction of more than one audit objective, it is practical to establish the audit objectives and then select audit procedures which avoid duplication of work.

SAMPLE AUDIT PROGRAM FOR CASH IN BANK

I. Audit Objectives:

A. Determine that cash recorded in books exists and is owned by the company (Existence).

B. Determine that cash transactions are recorded in the correct accounting period, i.e., that there is a proper cut-off of cash receipts and disbursements (Completeness).

C. Determine that balance sheet amounts include items in transit as well as cash on deposit with third parties (Completeness).

D. Determine that cash is properly classified in the balance sheet and that relevant disclosures are presented in the financial statement notes (Presentation and Disclosure).

II. Procedures:

A. With respect to the bank reconciliations prepared by accounting personnel:

> Trace book balances to general ledger control totals.

> Compare ending balances per the bank statements to the ending balances on the bank reconciliation.

> Verify the mathematical and clerical accuracy including checking extensions.

> Identify unusual reconciling items and obtain documentation to corroborate the validity of such items. *Note:* The current file of an auditor's audit documentation includes all working papers applicable to the current year under audit.

> Trace deposits in transit and outstanding checks to subsequent months' bank statements which are intercepted before accounting personnel have access to them.

> Inspect canceled checks for dates of cancellation in order to identify checks which were not recorded in the proper accounting period.

> Ascertain that checks listed as outstanding are in fact: (1) recorded in the proper time period, and (2) checks that have not cleared. Scrutinize data when outstanding checks have cleared to see if the books have been held open to improve ratios.

▶ Identify and investigate checks that are: (1) above limits pre-scribed by management, (2) drawn to "bearer," and (3) drawn payable to cash.

▶ Inquire about checks which have been outstanding for a more than reasonable time period.

▶ If balances have been confirmed with banks, compare confirmed balances with bank balances per the year-end bank statements.

B. With respect to listings of cash investments:

▶ Trace book balances to general ledger control accounts.

▶ Verify the accuracy of all extensions and footings.

▶ Consider confirming balances directly with bank personnel.

▶ Obtain and inspect passbooks and certificates of deposit.

▶ Recalculate income derived from cash investments and trace the income amounts to the books of original entry. Also, reconcile for reasonableness interest revenue amounts to the amount of cash investments.

▶ Consider using a custodian to maintain physical custody for safe-keeping and to guard against forgeries.

C. Prepare a bank transfer schedule which identifies:

▶ Name of disbursing bank

▶ Check number

▶ Dollar amount

▶ Date disbursement is recorded in books

▶ Name of receiving bank

▶ Date receipt is recorded in books

▶ Date receipt is recorded by bank

D. Perform cut-off test wherein transactions for the last few days of the year and the first few days of the next year are scrutinized.

E. Inspect bank statements in order to identify obvious erasures or alterations.

F. Inspect debit and credit memos and trace them to the bank statements.

G. Read financial statements and investment certificates for appropriate classification of cash balances.

H. With respect to cash on hand (i.e., petty cash funds):

  ▶ Determine the identity of all funds
  ▶ Select funds to be counted and list currency and coins by denomination; account for vouchers, stamps, and checks; trace fund balances to general ledger control accounts.

I. Investigate the reasons for delays in deposits.

J. Note unusual activity in inactive accounts since it may be indicative of cash being hidden.

K. In a cash-basis entity, reconcile sales with cash receipts.

L. List unusual cash receipts (e.g., currency receipts).

M. Examine third party endorsements by reviewing canceled checks.

SAMPLE AUDIT PROGRAM FOR TRADE ACCOUNTS AND NOTES RECEIVABLE

I. Audit Objectives:

A. Determine that the trade accounts and notes receivable represent bona fide receivables and are valued properly (Existence and Valuation).

B. Determine that the allowances for doubtful accounts are adequate and reasonable (Valuation).

C. Determine the propriety of disclosures pertaining to pledging, assigning, and discounting of receivables (Presentation and Disclosure).

D. Determine the correctness of the recorded interest income that is attributable to accounts and notes receivable (Completeness).

E. Determine that receivables are properly classified in the balance sheet (Presentation and Disclosure).

II. Audit Procedures:

A. Scan general ledger accounts in order to identify significant and unusual transactions.

B. Compare opening general ledger balances with closing general ledger balances of the prior period.

C. Perform analytical procedures by evaluating the relationships between: (1) receivables and sales and (2) notes receivable and interest income attributable thereon.

D. With respect to the aged trial balance prepared by accounting personnel:
   ▶ Verify extensions and footings.
   ▶ Trace the total of the aged trial balance to the general ledger control total.
   ▶ Trace selected entries on the aging schedule to respective accounts in the subsidiary ledger.
   ▶ Trace selected subsidiary ledger balances to the aging schedule.
   ▶ Verify extensions and footings in subsidiary ledger accounts
   ▶ Investigate negative (i.e., credit) balances.

E. Consider confirmation of account balances with customers:
   ▶ Select accounts for positive confirmation.

▶ Select accounts for negative confirmation.

▶ Control confirmation requests by mailing in internal audit department envelopes and with the return address of the internal audit department. Consider using a post office box to ensure that unauthorized individuals cannot tamper with responses.

▶ After 14 days, mail second requests to all those not replying to a positive request.

▶ Investigate all accounts for which envelopes are returned as undeliverable.

▶ Reconcile differences reported by customers.

▶ Review accounts of significant customers not replying to a second request by examining subsequent receipts and supporting documentation (i.e., remittance advices, invoices, and/or shipping documents) in order to corroborate that the amounts represent bona fide receivables for goods or services

▶ Prepare a schedule summarizing the receivable confirmations as follows:

	NO.	% DOLLAR	AMOUNT%
Total at Confirm Date			
Requested			
Total Positive Type			
Total at Confirm Date Requested			
Total Negative			
Type Total Requested			
Results			
Positive Exceptions Positive Clean			
Positive Nonreplies			
Total Positive Type			
Exceptions			
Total Negative Type Exceptions			

F. Examine cash receipts in subsequent periods in order to identify receivables which have not been recorded previously.

G. With respect to trade notes receivable, prepare or verify schedules and analyses which detail the following:
   ▶ Makers of the notes
   ▶ Dates the notes were made
   ▶ Due dates of the notes
   ▶ Original terms of repayment
   ▶ Any collateral
   ▶ Applicable interest rates
   ▶ Balances at the end of the prior accounting period
   ▶ Additions and repayments of principal

H. Inspect notes and confirm notes receivable discounted with banks.

I. Identify collateral and verify that such amounts are not recorded as assets.

J. Verify the accuracy of interest income, accrued interest, and unearned discount by recalculating such amounts.

K. Read pertinent documents, including the minutes of board meetings, in order to identify situations in which receivables have been pledged as collateral, assigned, or discounted and verify that such situations are disclosed in the financial statements.

L. Obtain evidence pertaining to related-party transactions which need to be disclosed in the financial statements.

M. With respect to the analysis of the allowance for doubtful accounts prepared by accounting personnel:
   ▶ Ascertain that write-offs have in fact been authorized
   ▶ Ascertain the reasonableness of the allowance
   ▶ Perform analytical procedures by comparing:

      – Accounts receivable to credit sales

      — Allowance for doubtful accounts to accounts receivable totals

      — Sales to sales returns and allowances

      — Doubtful accounts expense to net credit sales

      — Accounts receivable to total assets —Notes receivable totals to accounts receivable totals
   ▶ Consider differences between the book and tax basis for doubtful accounts expense.

SAMPLE AUDIT PROGRAM FOR INVENTORY

I. Audit Objectives:

A. Determine that inventory quantities properly include products, materials, and supplies on hand, in transit, in storage, and out on consignment to others (Existence, Completeness, and Valuation or Allocation).

B. Determine that inventory items are priced consistently in accordance with United States GAAP (Valuation or Allocation).

C. Determine that inventory listings are accurately compiled, extended, footed, and summarized and determine that the totals are properly reflected in the accounts (Existence, Completeness, and Valuation or Allocation).

D. Determine that excess, slow-moving, obsolete, and defective items are reduced to their net realizable value (Valuation or Allocation).

E. Determine that the financial statements include disclosure of any liens resulting from the pledging or assignment of inventories (Presentation and Disclosure).

II. Audit Procedures:

A. Review management's instructions pertaining to inventory counts and arrange to have sufficient internal audit personnel present to observe the physical count at major corporate locations. Keep in mind that all locations should be counted simultaneously in order to prevent substitution of items.

B. At each location where inventory is counted:
    ▶ Observe the physical inventory count, record test counts, and write an overall observation memo.
    ▶ Determine that prenumbered inventory tags are utilized.
    ▶ Test the control of inventory tags.
    ▶ Test shipping and receiving cut-offs.
    ▶ Discuss obsolescence and overstock with operating personnel.
    ▶ Verify that employees are indicating on inventory tags obsolete items.
    ▶ Note the condition of inventory.
    ▶ Note pledged or consigned inventory.

▶ Determine if any inventory is at other locations and consider confirmation or observation, if material.

▶ Determine that inventory marked for destruction is actually destroyed and is destroyed by authorized personnel.

C. Follow up all points that might result in a material adjustment.

D. Trace recorded test counts to the listings obtained from management, list all exceptions, and value the total effect.

E. Trace the receiving and shipping cut-offs obtained during the observation to the inventory records, accounts receivable records, and accounts payable records. Also trace inventory to production and sales.

F. Obtain a cut-off of purchases and sales subsequent to the audit date and trace to accounts receivable, accounts payable, and inventory records.

G. Note any sharp drop in market value relative to book value.

H. "Red flag" excessive product returns which might be indicative of quality problems. Returned merchandise should be warehoused apart from finished goods until quality control has tested the items. Are returns due to the salesperson overstocking the customer? Returns should be controlled as to actual physical receipt, and the reasons for the returns should be noted for analytical purposes.

I. Trace for possible obsolete merchandise that is continually carried on the books. For example, the author had a situation in which a company continued to carry obsolete goods on the books even though it wrote off only a small portion.

J. With respect to price tests of raw materials:
  ▶ Ascertain management's inventory pricing procedures
  ▶ Schedule, for a test of pricing, all inventory items in excess of a prescribed limit and sample additional items
  ▶ Inspect purchase invoices and trace to journal entries
  ▶ Inquire and investigate whether trade discounts, special rebates, and similar price reductions have been reflected in inventory prices
  ▶ Determine and test treatment of freight and duty costs
  ▶ If standard costs are utilized:

  Determine whether such costs differ materially from actual costs on a first-in, first-out basis.

Investigate variance accounts and compute the effect of the balances in such accounts on inventory prices.

Ascertain the policy and practice as to changes in standards.

With respect to changes during the period, investigate the effect on inventory pricing.

If process costs are used, trace selected quantities per the physical inventory to the departmental cost of production reports and determine that quantities have been adjusted to the physical inventory as of the date of the physical counts.

K. With respect to work-in-process and finished goods:
  ▶ Ascertain the procedures used in pricing inventory and determine the basis of pricing
  ▶ Review tax returns to determine that the valuation methods conform to those methods used for financial statement purposes
  ▶ On a test basis, trace unit costs per the physical inventory to the cost accounting records and perform the following:

    — Obtain, review, and compare the current-period and prior period's trial balances or tabulations of detailed components of production costs for the year; note explanations for apparent inconsistencies in classifications and significant fluctuations in amounts; ascertain that the cost classifications accumulated as production costs and absorbed in inventory are in conformity with United States GAAP.

    — Review computations of unit costs and costs credited against inventory and charged to cost of sales.

    — Review activity in the general ledger control accounts for raw materials, supplies, and work-in-process and finished goods inventories and investigate any significant and unusual entries or fluctuations.

    — Review labor and overhead allocations to inventory and cost of sales, compare to actual labor and overhead costs incurred, and ascertain that variances appear reasonable in amount and have been properly accounted for.

    — Trace who obtains the funds received from the sale of scrap.

SAMPLE AUDIT PROGRAM FOR FIXED ASSETS

I. Audit Objectives:

A. Determine that fixed assets exist (Existence or Occurrence).

B. Determine that fixed assets are owned by the entity (Rights and Obligations).

C. Determine that fixed asset accounts are recorded at historical cost (Valuation or Allocation).

D. Determine that depreciation is calculated and recorded in conformity with generally accepted accounting principles (Valuation or Allocation).

E. Determine that relevant disclosures are made in the financial statements (Presentation and Disclosure).

II. Audit Procedures:

A. With respect to the schedule of fixed assets prepared by accounting personnel:
   - Trace beginning balances to prior-year schedules
   - Trace ending balances to general ledger control accounts
   - Verify that additions are recorded at historical cost
   - Examine supporting documentation for asset additions, retirements, and dispositions: purchase contracts, canceled checks, invoices, purchase orders, receiving reports, retirement work orders, sale contracts, bills of sale, bills of lading, trade-in agreements
   - Verify that depreciation methods, estimated useful lives, and estimated salvage values are in accordance with United States generally accepted accounting principles (GAAP)
   - Recalculate gains and losses on dispositions of fixed assets in accordance with methods that are in conformity with United States GAAP

B. Determine that additions, retirements, and dispositions have been authorized by management.

C. Analyze repairs and maintenance accounts to ascertain the propriety of classification of transactions.

D. Tour facilities in order to physically inspect fixed assets. A lack of cleanliness and orderliness infer the possible existence of internal control problems.

E. To verify ownership, examine:
   - Personal property tax returns
   - Tide certificates
   - Insurance policies
   - Invoices
   - Purchase contracts

F. Read lease agreements and ascertain that the accounting treatment is in conformity with United States GAAP

G. Ascertain that obsolete assets are given proper accounting recognition. Trace salvage receipts to source.

H. Perform analytical procedures by comparing:
   - Dispositions of fixed assets to replacements
   - Depreciation and amortization expenses to the cost of fixed assets
   - Accumulated depreciation to the cost of fixed assets.

I. Read: (1) minutes of board meetings, (2) note agreements, and (3) purchase contracts to identify situations in which assets have been pledged as collateral.

SAMPLE AUDIT PROGRAM FOR PREPAID EXPENSES AND DEFERRED CHARGES

I. Audit Objectives:

A. Determine that balances represent proper charges against future operations and can reasonably be realized through future operations or are otherwise in conformity with United States GAAP (Valuation or Allocation).

B. Determine that additions during the audit period are proper charges to these accounts and represent actual cost (Existence or Occurrence and Valuation or Allocation).

C. Determine that amortization or write-offs against revenues in the current period and to date have been determined in a rational and consistent manner (Valuation or Allocation).

D. Determine that material items have been properly classified and disclosed in the financial statements (Presentation and Disclosure).

II. Audit Procedures:

A. Obtain or prepare a schedule of the prepaid and deferred items.

B. Perform analytical procedures by comparing current-period amounts to those of the prior period; investigate significant fluctuations.

C. With respect to prepaid insurance:
   ▶ Obtain a schedule of insurance policies, coverage, total premiums, prepaid premiums, and expense as of the audit date; note that some companies maintain an insurance register
   ▶ Verify the clerical and mathematical accuracy of schedules or insurance registers
   ▶ Trace schedule or register totals to trial balances and general ledger control accounts
   ▶ Inspect policies on hand and check details of schedules or registers
   ▶ Vouch significant premiums paid during the audit period
   ▶ Obtain confirmation directly from insurance brokers of premiums and other significant and relevant data

> ▶ Verify that proper accounting treatment is applied to advance or deposit premiums, as well as dividend or premium credits
>
> ▶ Test check calculations of prepaid premiums and investigate and determine the disposition of major differences.

D. With respect to prepaid taxes:

> ▶ Obtain or prepare an analysis of prepaid taxes, including taxes charged directly to expense accounts
>
> ▶ Verify the mathematical and clerical accuracy of the analysis
>
> ▶ Trace amounts on the analysis to the trial balance and pertinent general ledger control accounts
>
> ▶ Examine tax bills and receipts or other data which corroborate prepaid taxes
>
> ▶ Ascertain that prepaid tax accounts have been accounted for consistently in conformity with United States GAAP.

E. With respect to other major items:

> ▶ Review deferred expenses such as moving costs and determine:
>
> — What procedures are used to evaluate the future usefulness of the asset
>
> — How these assets will benefit the future
>
> ▶ Test the amortization of material prepaid or deferred items and trace to the income statement and general ledger accounts
>
> ▶ Inspect relevant documents

40

SAMPLE AUDIT PROGRAM FOR ACCOUNTS PAYABLE

I. Audit Objectives:

A. Determine that accounts payable in fact exist (Existence or Occurrence).

B. Determine that accounts payable represent authorized obligations of the entity (Existence or Occurrence).

C. Determine that accounts payable are properly classified in the financial statements (Presentation and Disclosure).

D. Determine that recorded accounts payable are complete (Completeness).

E. Determine that appropriate disclosures are included in the financial statements (Presentation and Disclosure).

II. Audit Procedures:

A. With respect to the schedule of accounts payable prepared by accounting personnel:
   - Verify mathematical accuracy of extensions and footings
   - Trace totals to general ledger control accounts
   - Trace selected individual accounts to the accounts payable subsidiary ledger
   - Trace individual account balances in the subsidiary ledger to the accounts payable schedule
   - Investigate accounts payable which are in dispute
   - Investigate any debit balances
   - Read minutes of board meetings to ascertain the existence of pledging agreements

B. Consider confirming accounts payable if there is: (1) poor internal control structure, or (2) suspicion of misstatement.

C. Search for unrecorded liabilities by
   - Examining receiving reports and matching them with invoices
   - Inspecting unprocessed invoices
   - Inspecting vendor's statements for unrecorded invoiced amounts

▶ Examine cash disbursements made in the period subsequent to year-end and examine supporting documentation in order to ascertain the appropriate cut-off for recording purposes.

D. With respect to obligations for payroll tax liabilities:
   ▶ Examine payroll tax deposit receipts
   ▶ Examine cash disbursements in the period subsequent to year-end to identify deposits that relate to prior period
   ▶ Reconcile general ledger control totals to payroll tax forms
   ▶ Trace liabilities for amounts withheld from employee checks to payroll registers, journals, and summaries
   ▶ Perform analytical procedures by comparing: Payroll tax expense to liabilities for payroll taxes, liability to accrued payroll taxes
   ▶ Reconcile calendar year payroll returns to fiscal year financial statements for payroll amounts

E. Reconcile vendor statements with accounts payable accounts.

F. Compare vendor invoices with purchase requisitions, purchase orders, and receiving reports for price and quantity.

G. Investigate unusually large purchases.

H. With respect to accrued expenses:
   ▶ Consider the existence of unasserted claims
   ▶ Obtain schedule of accrued expenses from accounting personnel
   ▶ Recalculate accruals after verifying the validity of assumptions utilized
   ▶ Perform analytical procedures by comparing current- and prior period accrued expenses
   ▶ Ascertain that accrued expenses are paid within a reasonable time after year-end
   ▶ Inquire of management and indicate all details of contingent or known liabilities arising from product warranties, guarantees, contests, advertising promotions, and dealer "arrangements or promises"
   ▶ Determine liability for expenses in connection with pending litigation:
      — Inquire of management
      — Confirm in writing with outside legal counsel

SAMPLE AUDIT PROGRAM FOR STOCKHOLDERS' EQUITY

I. Audit Objectives:

A. Determine that all stock transactions (including transactions involving warrants, options, and rights) have been authorized in accordance with management's plans (All Assertions Are Addressed).

B. Determine that equity transactions are properly classified in the financial statements (Presentation and Disclosure).

C. Determine that equity transactions have been recorded in the proper time period at the correct amounts (Existence or Occurrence, Completeness, and Presentation and Disclosure).

D. Determine that equity transactions are reflected in the financial statements in accordance with generally accepted accounting principles (Presentation and Disclosure).

II. Audit Procedures:

A. With respect to each class of stock, identify:
- Number of shares authorized
- Number of shares issued
- Number of shares outstanding
- Par or stated value
- Privileges
- Restrictions

B. With respect to the schedule of equity transactions prepared by accounting personnel:
- Trace opening balances of the current year to the balance sheet and ledger accounts as of the prior year's balance sheet date
- Account for all proceeds from stock issues by recomputing sales prices and relevant proceeds
- Verify the validity of the classification of proceeds between capital stock and additional paid-in capital
- Reconcile ending schedule balances with general ledger control totals

▶ Verify that equity transactions are not in conflict with the requirements of the corporate charter (or articles of incorporation), or with the applicable statutes of the state of incorporation

C. Account for all stock certificates that remain unissued at the end of the accounting period.

D. Examine stock certificate books or confirm stock register.

E. With respect to schedules of stock options and related stock option plans prepared by accounting personnel, verify:
   ▶ The date of the plan
   ▶ Class and number of shares reserved for the plan
   ▶ The accounting method used for determining option prices
   ▶ The names of individuals entitled to receive stock options
   ▶ The names of individuals to whom options have been granted
   ▶ The terms relevant to options that have been granted
   ▶ That measurement of stock options granted is in accordance with generally accepted accounting principles

F. With respect to stock subscriptions receivable:
   ▶ Ascertain that execution of such transactions is approved by appropriate personnel
   ▶ Verify that stock subscriptions receivable are properly classified in the financial statements

G. With respect to treasury stock:
   ▶ Verify the validity of treasury stock acquisitions by examining canceled checks and other corroborating documentation
   ▶ Inspect treasury stock certificates in order to ascertain their existence
   ▶ Obtain assurance that treasury stock certificates have been endorsed to the company or are in the company's name by physically inspecting the certificates
   ▶ Reconcile treasury stock totals to general ledger control accounts

H. With respect to retained earnings:
   ▶ Trace the opening balance in the general ledger to the ending balance in the general ledger of the prior period
   ▶ Analyze current-year transactions and obtain corroborating documentation for all or selected transactions

▶ Verify that current-year net income or loss has been reflected as a current-year transaction

▶ With respect to dividends declared and or paid:

— Ascertain the authorization of such dividends by reading the minutes of board meetings

— Examine canceled checks in support of dividend payments

— Verify the accuracy of dividend declarations and payments by recalculating such dividends

— Ascertain that prior-period adjustments have been given proper accounting recognition in accordance with generally accepted accounting principles

— Apply other appropriate procedures to determine the existence of restrictions on or appropriations of retained earnings

I. Ascertain that the financial statements include adequate disclosure of:

▶ Restrictions on stock

▶ Stock subscription rights

▶ Stock reservations

▶ Stock options and warrants

▶ Stock repurchase plans or obligations

▶ Preferred dividends in arrears

▶ Voting rights in the event of preferred dividend arrearages

▶ Liquidation preferences

▶ Other relevant items

SAMPLE AUDIT PROGRAM FOR SALES AND OTHER TYPES OF INCOME

I. Audit Objectives:

   A. Determine that proper income recognition is afforded ordinary sales transactions (Existence or Occurrence, Rights and Obligations, Valuation or Allocation, and Presentation and Disclosure).

   B. Determine that sales transactions have been recorded in the proper time period (Existence or Occurrence, Completeness, and Presentation and Disclosure).

   C. Determine that all types of revenues are properly classified and disclosed in the financial statements (Valuation or Allocation and Presentation and Disclosure).

II. Audit Procedures:

   A. Trace sales and cash receipts journal totals to relevant general ledger control accounts.

   B. Trace sales and cash receipts journal entries to applicable subsidiary ledger accounts.

   C. Verify the mathematical accuracy of footings and extensions in sales and cash receipts journals.

   D. Perform analytical procedures by:
- Comparing current- and prior-period sales, returns and allowances, discounts, and gross profit percentages
- Comparing the current period items referred to above to anticipated results (i.e., budgeted amounts)
- Compare company statistics (e.g., gross profit percentage) to industry standards
- Investigate any significant or unexplained fluctuations

   E. With respect to consignment shipments to others:
- Examine applicable consignment agreements
- Verify that consignment transactions are afforded proper accounting treatment in accordance with generally accepted accounting principles

F. Ascertain that sales to related parties are accounted for at arm's length terms.

G. Perform sales and inventory cut-off tests at the end of the fiscal year.

H. Verify by recalculation that the following have been properly recorded and disclosed:
- Dividend income
- Interest income
- Gains on dispositions of marketable securities
- Gains on dispositions of fixed assets
- Increases in investment accounts reflecting the equity method of accounting
- Other or miscellaneous income accounts

SAMPLE AUDIT PROGRAM FOR EXPENSE ITEMS

I. Audit Objectives:

A. Determine that expenses are recorded in the proper time period (Existence or Occurrence and Completeness).

B. Determine that expenses have been properly classified and disclosed in the financial statements (Presentation and Disclosure).

C. Determine that expense items are recognized in accordance with generally accepted accounting principles (Valuation or Allocation).

II. Audit Procedures:

A. Trace cash disbursements journal totals to relevant general ledger control accounts.

B. Trace cash disbursements journal items to relevant subsidiary ledgers (e.g., payroll subledger).

C. Verify the mathematical accuracy of footings and extensions of relevant journals.

D. Perform analytical procedures by:
- ▶ Comparing current- and prior-period expense items
- ▶ Comparing the current-period expense items to anticipated results (i.e., budgeted amounts)
- ▶ Compare the current-period expense items to industry standards
- ▶ Relate various expense items to gross sales or revenue by means of percentages
- ▶ Investigate any significant or unexplained fluctuations
- ▶ Vouch bills on a sampling basis

E. Consider analyzing the following accounts, which are often subject to intentional or unintentional misstatement:
- ▶ Depreciation and amortization
- ▶ Taxes:

  — Real estate

  — Personal property

  — Income

  — Payroll

  — Rent
- ▶ Insurance
- ▶ Bad debts
- ▶ Interest
- ▶ Professional fees
- ▶ Officers' salaries
- ▶ Directors' fees
- ▶ Travel and entertainment
- ▶ Research and development
- ▶ Charitable contributions
- ▶ Repairs and maintenance

F. With respect to payroll:
- ▶ Search for fictitious employees
- ▶ Determine improper alterations of amounts
- ▶ Verify that proper tax deductions are taken
- ▶ Examine time cards and trace to payroll records in order to verify the proper recording of employee hours.

> ▶ Verify the accuracy of pay rates by obtaining a list of authorized pay rates from the personnel department.
> ▶ Review the adequacy of internal controls relating to hiring, overtime, and retirement.
> ▶ Determine if proper payroll forms exist such as W-4s and I-9s.

SAS 99—Consideration of Fraud in a Financial Statement Audit

What is the difference between error and fraud?

The distinction between error and fraud is dependent on whether the underlying action that results in financial statement misstatement is intentional or unintentional. Error refers to unintentional misstatements or omissions of financial statement amounts or disclosures—for example, misinterpretation, mistakes, and use of incorrect accounting estimates. Fraud, on the other hand, refers to acts that are intentional.

What types of misstatements are relevant to an auditor's consideration of fraud?

▶ Misstatements arising from fraudulent financial reporting, including manipulation, falsification, or alteration of accounting records or supporting documents, and intentional misapplication of accounting principles, practices, and methods

▶ Misstatements arising from misappropriation of assets (i.e., defalcation), including outright theft, embezzlement schemes, and causing an entity to pay for goods or services that the entity does not actually receive

What conditions are usually present when fraud occurs?

▶ Pressure or incentive to commit fraud
▶ Opportunity to perpetrate fraud
▶ Ability to rationalize or justify committing fraud

Is an auditor responsible for detecting fraud in a financial statement audit?

An auditor is responsible for planning and performing a financial statement audit in order to obtain reasonable, but not absolute, assurance about whether the financial statements are free of material misstatement, whether caused by fraud (or error).

Note: An auditor is not framed as, or normally expected to be, an expert in authentication. Accordingly, an auditor might not discover material misstatements caused by fraud that is concealed through falsified (forged) documents. Collusion might also prevent an auditor's detection.

Because of the characteristics of fraud, the auditor is advised to exercise professional judgment. Accordingly, the auditor should have a questioning mind and critically assess evidence obtained throughout the conduct of the audit.

What is meant by brainstorming?

SAS 99 requires members of the audit team to discuss the potential for material misstatement due to fraud. Brainstorming, or exchange of ideas, is therefore emphasized. Audit team members should brainstorm about

- ▶ How and where the financial statements might be susceptible to material misstatement due to fraud
- ▶ How management could perpetrate and conceal fraudulent financial reporting
- ▶ How an entity's assets could be misappropriated
- ▶ The need to emphasize professional skepticism throughout the audit
- ▶ The risk of management override of internal controls
- ▶ How the audit team might respond to the susceptibility of the financial statements to material misstatement caused by fraud

In general, how may an auditor identify risks that may result in material misstatement caused by fraud?

An auditor should consider the attributes of the risk of material misstatement caused by fraud:

- ▶ Type of risk—that is, whether the risk involves fraudulent financial reporting or misappropriation of assets
- ▶ Significance of risk—that is, whether it is of a magnitude that could result in material misstatement
- ▶ Likelihood of risk
- ▶ Pervasiveness of risk—that is, is the risk isolated to a particular assertion, account, or class of transaction, or does the risk have a potentially pervasive effect on the financial statements?

How should an auditor respond to the results of the assessment of the risk of material misstatement caused by fraud?

An auditor generally responds to the risk of material misstatement caused by fraud by:

- Developing a response that has an overall effect on the conduct of the audit
- Modifying the nature, extent, and timing of specific auditing procedures
- Performing additional auditing procedures to address the risk of material misstatement due to fraud arising from management override of internal controls

How might the risk of material misstatement caused by fraud have an overall effect on the audit?

Judgments about the risk of material misstatement caused by fraud may have an overall effect on the audit in the following ways:

- Assignment of personnel—The knowledge, skill, and ability of audit personnel should be commensurate with the assessed level of risk
- Accounting principles—The auditor should be more skeptical about management's selection and application of accounting principles, practices, and methods
- Predictability of auditing procedures—The auditor should incorporate an element of unpredictability in selecting auditing procedures performed from year to year

What procedures should be performed to address the risk of management override of internal controls?

The auditor should examine journal entries and other adjustments. More specifically, the auditor should:

- Obtain an understanding of the financial reporting process and the relevant internal controls.
- Identify and select journal entries and other adjustments for substantive testing.
- Determine the timing of substantive tests, with special focus on journal entries and other adjustments made at the end of the reporting period.
- Make inquiries of individuals involved in the financial reporting process about inappropriate or unusual activity concerning the processing of journal entries and other adjustments.

What should an auditor be aware of when evaluating audit evidence?

It is important to keep in mind that the assessment of the risk of material misstatement caused by fraud is not a onetime assessment, but rather should be ongoing throughout the conduct of the audit.-

Accordingly, on an ongoing basis, the auditor should watch out for the following:

- Discrepancies in the accounting records
- Conflicting or missing evidential matter
- Problematic or unusual relationships between management and the auditor

The auditor should also:

- Evaluate whether analytical procedures in the substantive testing and overall review stages of the audit indicate previously unrecognized risks of material misstatement caused by fraud.
- At or near the end of fieldwork, evaluate the accumulated results of audit tests to determine the effect on the auditor's earlier risk assessment.

What actions should an auditor take if he or she believes that financial statement misstatements are or may be caused by fraud?

If the auditor believes that the effect of the misstatement is immaterial, he or she should nevertheless evaluate the implications, especially those dealing with the organizational position of the individual(s) involved.

If the auditor believes that the effect of the misstatement is material, or is unable to determine the materiality of the misstatement, the following actions are appropriate:

- Undertake to obtain additional evidential matter in order to ascertain whether material fraud has occurred, or is likely to have occurred, and if so, its related effects on the financial statements as well as the auditor's report.
- Consider the possible effects on other aspects of the audit.
- Discuss the matter as well as the approach for further investigation with an appropriate level of management that is at least one level above those involved, and with senior management, and the audit committee.
- Consider whether it is appropriate to advise the client to consult with its legal counsel.

What communications concerning fraud or its possibility are necessary?

An appropriate level of management should be notified if the auditor determines that there is evidence of fraud, even if the fraud is inconsequential.

The audit committee should be notified directly if the auditor determines that there is:

- Fraud involving senior management
- Fraud that results in material misstatement in the financial statements

If the auditor concludes that identified fraud risk factors have continuing internal control implications, the auditor should determine whether such factors represent reportable conditions requiring communication to senior management or the audit committee.

Although an auditor is generally precluded from communicating with nonclient personnel about fraud, he or she is permitted to disclose such information when:

- Permitted by law or regulatory requirements
- A predecessor auditor communicates with a successor auditor pursuant to the provisions of SAS 84
- Responding to a subpoena
- Required to notify a funding agency or other specified agency pursuant to requirements for the audits of entities that receive governmental financial assistance

Does SAS 99 contain any specific documentation requirements?

The auditor is required to document the following.

- The details of the required brainstorming.
- The procedures performed to identify and assess the risks of material misstatement caused by fraud.
- Specific risks of material misstatement caused by fraud that the auditor identified as well as a description of the auditor's response thereto.
- The basis for the conclusion, if the auditor has not identified in particular circumstance improper revenue recognition as a risk of material misstatement caused by fraud.
- The results of the procedures to further address the risk of management override of internal controls.
- Other conditions and results of analytical procedures that led the auditor to believe that additional audit procedures were necessary, as well as any further responses the auditor considered necessary.
- The nature of the communications concerning fraud made to management, the audit committee, and others.

Does SAS 99 provide lists of risk factors relating to misstatements arising from fraudulent financial reporting and misappropriation of assets?

The following list of risk factors is derived from the Appendix to SAS 99.

Risk factors relating to misstatements arising from fraudulent financial reporting

Incentives/Pressures

A. Financial stability or profitability is threatened by economic, industry, or entity operating conditions, such as (or as indicated by):

1. High degree of competition or market saturation, accompanied by declining margins

2. High vulnerability to rapid changes, such as changes in technology, product obsolescence, or interest rates

3. Significant declines in customer demand and increasing business failures in either the industry or overall economy

4. Operating losses making the threat of bankruptcy, foreclosure, or hostile takeover imminent

5. Recurring negative cash flows from operations or an inability to generate cash flows from operations while reporting earnings and earnings growth

6. Rapid growth or unusual profitability, especially compared to that of other companies in the same industry

7. New accounting, statutory, or regulatory requirements

B. Excessive pressure exists for management to meet the requirements or expectations of third parties due to the following:

1. Profitability or trend level expectations of investment analysts, institutional investors, significant creditors, or other external parties (particularly expectations that are unduly aggressive — or unrealistic), including expectations created by management in, for example, overly optimistic press releases or annual report messages

2. Need to obtain additional debt or equity financing to stay competitive—including financing of major research and development or capital expenditures

3. Marginal ability to meet exchange listing requirements or debt repayment or other debt covenant requirements

4. Perceived or real adverse effects of reporting poor financial results on significant pending transactions, such as business combinations or contract awards

C Information available indicates that management or the board of directors' personal financial situation is threatened by the entity's financial performance arising from the following:

1. Significant financial interests in the entity

2. Significant portions of their compensation (for example, bonuses, stock options, and earn-out arrangements) being contingent upon achieving aggressive targets for stock price, operating results, financial position, or cash flow

3. Personal guarantees of debts of the entity

D. There is excessive pressure on management or operating personnel to meet financial targets setup by the board of directors or management, including sales or profitability incentive goals.

Opportunities

A. The nature of the industry or the entity's operations provides opportunities to engage in fraudulent financial reporting that can arise from the following:

1. Significant related-party transactions not in the ordinary course of business or with related entities not audited or audited by another firm

2. A strong financial presence or ability to dominate a certain industry sector that allows the entity to dictate terms or conditions to suppliers or customers that may result in inappropriate or non-arm's-length transactions

3. Assets, liabilities, revenues, or expenses based on significant estimates that involve subjective judgments or uncertainties that are difficult to corroborate

4. Significant, unusual, or highly complex transactions, especially those close to period end that pose difficult "substance over form" questions

5. Significant operations located or conducted across international borders in jurisdictions where differing business environments and cultures exist

6. Significant bank accounts or subsidiary or branch operations in tax-haven jurisdictions for which there appears to be no clear business justification

B. There is ineffective monitoring of management as a result of the following:

1. Domination of management by a single person or small group (in a nonowner-managed business) without compensating controls

2. Ineffective board of directors or audit committee oversight over the financial reporting process and internal control

C There is a complex or unstable organizational structure, as evidenced by the following:

1. Difficulty in determining the organization or individuals that have controlling interest in the entity
2. Overly complex organizational structure involving unusual legal entities or managerial lines of authority
3. High turnover of senior management, counsel, or board members

D. Internal control components are deficient as a result of the following

Inadequate monitoring of controls, including automated controls and controls over interim financial reporting (where external reporting is required)

High turnover rates or employment of ineffective accounting, internal audit, or information technology staff

Ineffective accounting and information systems, including situations involving reportable conditions

Attitudes/Rationalizations

▶ Ineffective communication, implementation, support, or enforcement of the entity's values or ethical standards by management or the communication of inappropriate values or ethical standards
▶ Nonfinancial management's excessive participation in or preoccupation with the selection of accounting principles or the determination of significant estimates
▶ Known history of violations of securities laws or other laws and regulations, or claims against the entity, its senior management, or board members alleging fraud or violations of laws and regulations
▶ Excessive interest by management in maintaining or increasing the entity's stock price or earnings trend
▶ A practice by management of committing to analysts, creditors, and other third parties to achieve aggressive or unrealistic forecasts
▶ Management failing to correct known reportable conditions on a timely basis
▶ An interest by management in employing inappropriate means to minimize reported earnings for tax-motivated reasons
▶ Recurring attempts by management to justify marginal or inappropriate accounting on the basis of materiality
▶ The relationship between management and the current or predecessor auditor is strained, as exhibited by the following
▶ Frequent disputes with the current or predecessor auditor on accounting, auditing, or reporting matters

▶ Unreasonable demands on the auditor, such as unreasonable time constraints regarding the completion of the audit or the issuance of the auditor's report

▶ Formal or informal restrictions on the auditor that inappropriately limit access to people or information or the ability to communicate effectively with the board of directors or audit committee

▶ Domineering management behavior in dealing with the auditor, especially involving attempts to influence the scope of the auditor's work or the selection or continuance of personnel assigned to or consulted on the audit engagement

Risk factors relating to misstatements arising from misappropriation of assets

Incentives/Pressures

A. Personal financial obligations may create *pressure* on management or employees with access to cash or other assets susceptible to theft to misappropriate those assets.

B. Adverse relationships between the entity and employees with access to cash or other assets susceptible to theft may motivate those employees to misappropriate those assets. For example, adverse relationships may be created by the following:

    1. Known or anticipated future employee layoffs

    2. Recent or anticipated changes to employee compensation or benefit plans

    3. Promotions, compensation, or other rewards - -inconsistent with expectations

Opportunities

A. Certain characteristics or circumstances may increase the susceptibility of assets to misappropriation. For example, opportunities to misappropriate assets increase when there are the following:

    1. Large amounts of cash on hand or processed

    2. Inventory items that are small in size, of high value, or in high demand

    3. Easily convertible assets, such as bearer bonds, diamonds, or computer chips

    4. Fixed assets that are small in size, marketable, or lacking observable identification of ownership

B. Inadequate internal control over assets may increase the susceptibility of misappropriation of those assets. For example, misappropriation of assets may occur because there is the following:

1. Inadequate segregation of duties or independent checks
2. Inadequate management oversight of employees responsible for assets, for example, inadequate supervision or monitoring of remote locations
3. Inadequate job applicant screening of employees with access to assets
4. Inadequate recordkeeping with respect to assets
5. Inadequate system of authorization and approval of transactions (for example, in purchasing)
6. Inadequate physical safeguards over cash, investments, inventory, or fixed assets
7. Lack of complete and timely reconciliations of assets
8. Lack of timely and appropriate documentation of transactions, for example, credits for merchandise returns
9. Lack of mandatory vacations for employees performing key control functions
10. Inadequate management understanding of information technology, which enables information technology employees to perpetrate a misappropriation
11. Inadequate access controls over automated records, including controls over and review of computer systems event logs.

Attitudes/Rationalizations

Risk factors reflective of employee attitudes/rationalizations that allow them to justify misappropriations of assets, are generally not susceptible to observation by the auditor. Nevertheless, the auditor who becomes aware of the existence of such information should consider it in identifying the risks of material misstatement arising from misappropriation of assets. For example, auditors may become aware of the following attitudes or behavior of employees who have access to assets susceptible to misappropriation:

▶ Disregard for the need for monitoring or reducing risks related to misappropriations of assets
▶ Disregard for internal control over misappropriation of assets by overriding existing controls or by failing to correct known internal control deficiencies
▶ Behavior indicating displeasure or dissatisfaction with the company or its treatment of the employee

▶ Changes in behavior or lifestyle that may indicate assets have been misappropriated

Techniques for fraud prevention

It's not sufficient just to detect and investigate fraud. Your company must have a strategy to fight fraud. A well-rounded anti-fraud program will have taken measures that will prevent fraud. Once this is implemented, everything else will fall into place. Here is how you can develop strategies that will work for you. One of the biggest challenges for the fraud examiner is to persuade management that the risks of fraud cannot be underestimated. Those who have not suffered from fraud previously will be unaware of the risks and costs. Management may simply think in terms of the direct financial costs but need to be encouraged to look further. These include:

▶ Consequential loss
▶ Legal and investigative costs
▶ Regulatory fines
▶ Management time
▶ Increased insurance premiums
▶ Loss of key staff and customers
▶ Increased cost of/inability to raise new finance

Fraud can never be eliminated from business entirely, simply because collusion can always overcome normal organizational controls. Combating fraud needs a different and fresh approach that should cover all aspects of the fraud cycle:

▶ Fraud deterrence and prevention
▶ Fraud detection
▶ Fraud investigation

An approach is recommended that includes the following components:

▶ Establish the right culture
▶ Establish a whistle-blowing policy
▶ Identify the risks
▶ Implement effective controls
▶ Increase awareness of the risks
▶ Plan for the worst
▶ Recruit the right people
▶ Search for suspicious transactions

Recruitment

Before a company opens its doors to new employees, managers should stop and ask themselves "Do I really know this person well enough to trust them with my money, confidential information, and above all my reputation?" Many companies believe that their recruitment procedures will deal with this question. A Mori poll (www.mori.com) revealed that:

- ▶ 30% of employees admitted to lying while applying for jobs;
- ▶ 18% of employees think it is necessary to exaggerate on their curriculum vitae;
- ▶ 34% of managers do not check the background of applicants; and
- ▶ 36% of organizations state that untruths on curriculum vitas (CVs) cost them significant time and money.

It goes to show that companies should check each new candidate thoroughly. The more senior the position, the more thorough this checking should be. Senior staff has more opportunity to commit fraud as they are in positions of trust and tend to have the ability to authorize payments and approve contracts. They are also more likely to commit frauds that can permanently damage their organization.

On-going process

Vetting is not only for new employees. It should be an on-going process across the whole workforce. For example:

- ▶ What if an individual commenced employment many years ago when vetting was less rigorous?
- ▶ What if an individual's circumstances have changed such that they now find themselves under severe financial pressures?

When staff with more than ten years of service is responsible for one-third of all frauds, you can easily see why it is important to adopt continual vetting procedures. Here are the Do's and Don'ts as part of their hiring process:

DO	DON'T
Ask all potential employees to complete a detailed application form	Rely only on a curriculum vitae provided by the applicant
Look for gaps in employment history	Limit checks to, say, the last ten years only
Request written references and check by telephone	Accept "to whom it may concern" reference letters

DO	DON'T
Check all qualifications	Accept copy certificates
Carry out in-depth due diligence in relation to senior employees	Assume a previous employer has carried out full and proper due diligence
If possible, obtain details of criminal records	Accept verbal representations at face value
Carry out checks on temporary and contract staff as well	.

Codes of conduct

The aim of a corporate policy is to demonstrate to both employees and the outside world that the company is taking the threat of dishonesty, fraud, and theft seriously. By issuing a detailed policy, it clearly sets out what is considered to be dishonest and warns any potential wrongdoers that the consequences of being caught will be serious. The effect therefore will be to deter any potential wrongdoers thus resulting in reduced losses from any wrongdoing and reduced costs in respect of investigating any wrongdoing.

There should be a general policy statement on ethics and the company's attitude toward dishonesty, fraud, and theft. Other matters that should be considered include:

▶ Does the policy make a distinction between fraud committed by employees, suppliers, customers etc.?

▶ Is the policy communicated to all staff (e.g., when they are recruited, induction training, extranet etc.)?

▶ Is staff required to confirm that they understand the policy and that they have complied with it in all respects?

▶ Does the policy make it clear that it applies to all staff including directors?

▶ Does the policy apply to all subsidiaries, including those abroad?

Definition of fraud

The policy should include a clear definition of what is regarded as fraud or theft. For example:

▶ Does the policy set out the company's attitude toward client entertaining and gifts and what action needs to be undertaken on receipt of these?

▶ Does the policy quantify what constitutes fraud or dishonesty? For example, an overstatement of expenses by $1 might not be considered to be fraud, but continuously over-claiming expenses by $1 might be considered dishonest.

▶ Does the policy distinguish between the seriousness of different offenses?

▶ Does the policy include a statement in respect to the misstatement of financial statements or destruction of accounting records?

▶ Does the policy include a statement in respect to conflicts of interest?

▶ What policies are in place to inform customers/suppliers that a code of conduct is in operation?

Whistleblowing policy

When appointed to carry out investigations, the first point of call are members of the staff. The reason for this is that they are the "eyes and ears" of a company. They know exactly what frauds are going on and who is doing it. They are an extremely valuable resource that companies are failing to utilize. What makes things worse is that if used properly they could have stopped the fraud much earlier. An even better source of information for the investigator is an ex-employee as they have less to lose by blowing the whistle. For those current members of staff that do blow the whistle, the consequences can be disastrous. Far from being hailed as corporate heroes and saving the business from potential financial ruin, three out of four whistleblowers are sidelined or their careers blighted by their honest actions. Employers should be encouraging whistleblowers to come forward as the quicker a business can spot fraud, the better. Not only does early detection diminish the damage to a firm's reputation, but it wastes less of management's time, and ultimately costs the business less. This is why having a robust whistleblowing policy in place is good practice. Having such a policy might also discourage potential whistleblowers from approaching the press as a first resort. In addition, businesses need to engender a culture in which employees believe their concerns will be taken seriously, and that the protection afforded by the law and policies is real.

Increase awareness of risks

Fraud examiners have a wealth of experience that has been obtained through investigation. One of the positive steps that they can take is to pass this experience back to company management and staff through an education process. Most employees and management will be unaware of the risks faced by their organization. Without knowing what the risks are, they will be unable to take corrective action.

The methods that the fraud examiner can take to increase awareness of the risks faced by companies include:

▶ Lectures to management and staff on general fraud awareness.

▶ Presentation of case studies.

▶ Use of the company intranet.

▶ Articles in company magazines.

Implement controls

Once a fraud examiner has carried out the above steps, she will then be in a position to implement specific controls to prevent fraud. If the right candidates have been recruited and the company has an effective code of conduct and whistleblowing process, the need for effective controls will be less urgent. The opposite is true if the company has not recruited the right candidates or established a code of conduct and whistleblowing policy. In fact, without having dealt with the issues referred to above, a company will find that implementing effective controls may not have the desired effect as staff will work out how to defeat these controls.

The fraud examiner will first want to identify the high-risk areas. This can be achieved through a workshop attended by management and staff from different areas of the business (e.g., accounting, warehouse, operations, marketing, etc). Each will have a different perspective that may be counter to another attendees' perspective. Having identified the risk areas (e.g. procurement of IT equipment etc.), the fraud examiner will want to review the following:

- ▶ Lack of segregation of duties
- ▶ Lack of physical safeguards
- ▶ Lack of independent checks
- ▶ Lack of authorization
- ▶ Overriding of existing controls
- ▶ Ineffectiveness of existing controls
- ▶ Inadequacy of the accounting system

Data mining

Data is a fundamental element in any organization's ability to manage its business; it is collected from a wide variety of sources, stored on many different systems, and is regularly used for marketing and sales activities. However, the use of this data in fraud detection is frequently overlooked.

The likelihood of identifying potentially fraudulent activity can be significantly enhanced through the regular application of data mining tools and techniques, although these are not foolproof and must be run in conjunction with other activities designed to reduce the threat of fraud.

Technology as a tool

People commit frauds, but as technology plays an increasingly important role in business life, the fraudster often leaves warning signals of his activity in an organization's systems.

Each transaction will leave a trail. Increasingly, in order to enhance the way an organization does business, databases have been developed to store huge amounts of transactional and standing data from accounting, sales, purchasing, and payroll functions. This is used for marketing, forecasting, and reporting but rarely for detecting and predicting fraud. Also, this data can be a key factor in developing and implementing a fraud risk management strategy.

Use of spreadsheets

Data mining in its simplest form may take the form of a "sorted" Excel spreadsheet where the fraud examiner is trying to identify the largest suppliers or customers. A further development of this is to track expenditure with the largest suppliers over time. This can be achieved using pivot tables in Excel followed by the charting function. Charting expenditure over time identified a single payment of over a specified limit to a particular supplier. Further investigation may reveal that it may have been paid to a fictitious company.

Use of databases

The next stage in data mining is the use of databases to run complex queries. Microsoft Access is an extremely powerful tool which many fraud examiners will be able to use. More complex databases include ACL and WinIdea. These may require specialist knowledge. However, they can analyze large amounts of data and produce complex queries that can be automated. The following chart illustrates that data mining has identified a series of transactions just above $50,000, which is the authorization limit for the company.

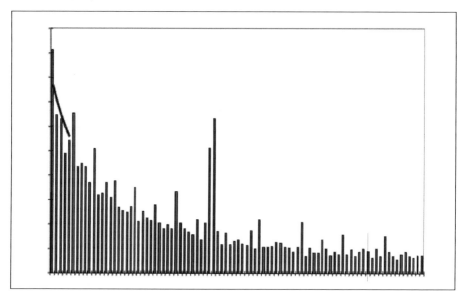

Databases can also be used to identify suspicious transactions around points in time.

Fraud response plan

When fraud comes to light, the actions taken in the first few hours, days, or weeks will be key in limiting the damage that is done to the company. It is no good "making it up as you go along" and "proper planning prevents poor performance." The plan should identify at least one individual to whom fraud or suspicion of fraud should be reported. Those concerned should then receive proper training and guidance on what to do once the fraud has been reported.

These individuals should always be contactable (i.e., 24/7) as a fraud can come to light at anytime. Employees will need to know whom to contact and how to contact them. Also, many frauds are now conducted on an international scale and company operations may be carried out abroad. In a move to make businesses efficient, multi-shifts means there is 24-hour production in some businesses.

The individuals chosen to sit on the fraud response team will need to have appropriate seniority and independence - they should not be in a position where a conflict of interest could arise.

After the initial report of fraud, the company may consider creating a larger group that would be responsible for managing the investigation or other response. If this is the case, then plans will have to be put into place to contact the other members of the group to discuss next steps. The plan should therefore consider:

- ▶ What constitutes a fraud which requires the attention of the larger group?
- ▶ Who makes the decision as to whether the larger group should be consulted?
- ▶ When should the group meet and report by?

Powers of the group

The powers of the group should be set out in writing so that it is clear they have the power to act. The powers should be sufficient to ensure that they can carry out their role without hindrance or delay, both internally or externally. The group may need to consult the board of directors and should have the ability to do so directly.

Responsibilities of the group

The outcome of an investigation may vary depending on the size of the fraud, who was involved, or how it was perpetrated. The group will therefore have to make an initial assessment as to what action would be desirable. The group will have to take action to:

- ▶ Suspend or dismiss the persons involved

▶ Prevent further losses
▶ Recovery of any losses incurred
▶ Pursue criminal action

The group may also have to consider what should be communicated and to whom. It will be almost impossible to keep the details of the fraud from other members of staff. Once staff becomes aware of the fraud, it will then spread to the press, investors, unions, customers, and suppliers. Therefore, the group will have to determine:

▶ Whether the PR department has been briefed on how to respond to press enquiries.
▶ At what stage investors will be informed.
▶ Whether unions should be regularly briefed.
▶ How suppliers will be informed if one of their employees is involved.

If the company has insurance coverage, the insurance company will need to be informed at an early stage to ensure that coverage applies and that, if it wishes, it can involve its own professional advisors in the investigation process.

Whom to contact for assistance

At some stage during the investigation process, it is likely that outside assistance will be required. At the lowest level, this may be a locksmith who is required to change office locks on a Sunday night. Details of any individual or entity that is likely to be able to assist should be obtained before it is required - this includes contact details out of normal working hours.

Contact with the police

Companies have historically wanted to avoid informing the police as they are afraid of any adverse publicity. Once reported to the police, directors believe that they will lose control of the investigation. This may have been true in the past but the police are now better equipped to investigate fraud. There are also positive aspects to reporting fraud to the police. It sends a very strong sign to the workforce and can act as a strong deterrent to any potential fraudsters. If they think that the company will prosecute them, they could then lose everything else, including family and friends. The company will therefore have to determine what its attitude toward reporting offenses to the police is. It will have to separately establish its obligations in relation to regulators.

CHAPTER 3

Statistical Sampling in Tests of Controls

Tests of controls

SAS 55 defines tests of controls as tests directed toward the design or operation of an internal control to assess its effectiveness in preventing or detecting material misstatements in financial statement assertion. Inquiry of company personnel, inspection of client documents and records, observation of client activities, and reperformance of controls represent some of the procedures used in performing tests of controls. In performing tests of controls, the auditor seeks answers to the following questions:

- ▶ Who performed the control?
- ▶ When was the control performed?
- ▶ How was the control performed?
- ▶ Was the control consistently applied?

Statistical sampling

Statistical sampling helps the auditor to design an efficient sample, to measure the sufficiency of the evidence obtained, and to evaluate the sample results. The standard of field work requires auditors to obtain sufficient competent evidence. Sufficiency relates to the design and size of the sample. Statistical sampling permits the auditors to measure sampling risk and therefore to design more efficient samples, that is, samples of a size necessary to provide sufficient evidence. *Note:* The size of the population has a very small effect on the required sample size when the population is large. Tables are available for smaller population sizes providing appropriate smaller sample sizes.

The results of statistical (probability) sampling are objective and subject to the laws of probability. Hence, sampling risk can be quantified and controlled, and the degree of reliability desired (the confidence level) can be specified. Sampling risk is the risk that the sample selected does not represent the population.

There are a number of statistical (probability or random) sampling methods that will aid auditors in performing tests of controls. They include attribute sampling, variables sampling, discovery sampling, multistage sampling, and stratified sampling. Of course, judgement (nonstatistical) sampling may also be undertaken. Statistical sampling is applicable to both tests of control (attribute sampling) and substantive testing (variable sampling).

Sampling risk

Sampling risk is the probability that a properly drawn sample may not be representative of the population; that is, the conclusions drawn from the sample may differ from those drawn if all the items in the population are examined. Sampling risk is to be measured and controlled. *Note:* Nonsampling risk involves all aspects of audit risk not caused by sampling, such as the auditor's inability to recognize noncompliance or the application of inappropriate procedures. The auditor controls sampling risk by specifying the acceptable level when developing the sampling plan.

(1) For tests of controls, sampling risk has the following aspects:

▶ The risk of assessing control risk too low is the risk that the assessed level of control risk based on the sample is less than the true operating effectiveness of internal control. This risk relates to audit effectiveness and *could cause audit failure*. Control risk is the risk that controls do not prevent or detect material misstatements on a timely basis.

▶ The risk of assessing control risk too high is the risk that the assessed level of control risk based on the sample is greater than the true operating effectiveness of internal control. This risk concerns audit efficiency and is likely to result in greater audit effort. The auditor's overassessment of control risk may lead to an unnecessary extension of the substantive tests. This risk is also termed a Type I error or Alpha risk.

(2) For substantive tests of account balances, sampling risk has the following aspects:

▶ The risk of incorrect acceptance, a Type II error or Beta risk, is the risk that the sample supports the conclusion that the recorded account balance is not materially misstated when it is materially misstated. This risk relates to audit effectiveness and could cause an audit failure.

▶ The risk of incorrect rejection, a Type I error or Alpha risk, is the risk that the sample supports the conclusion that the recorded account balance is materially misstated when it is not materially misstated. After an incorrect rejection, the client would likely maintain that the balance is properly stated. The auditor would then expend more audit effort, ultimately to conclude that the balance is fairly stated. This risk relates to the efficiency, not the effectiveness, of the audit. If the cost and effort of selecting additional sample items are low, a higher risk of incorrect rejection may be acceptable.

(3) The confidence level, also termed the reliability level, is the complement of the applicable sampling risk factor. Thus, for a test of controls, if the risk of assessing control risk too low is 5%, the auditor's confidence level is 95% (100% - 5%). For a substantive test, if the risk of incorrect rejection is 5%, the auditor's confidence level is 95% (100% - 5%).

Methods of choosing a random sample

A random sample may be chosen through a random sampling table or systematic sampling.

Random number sampling technique (using a random number table)

In random sampling, there is an equal probability of each sampling unit being chosen. Further, every possible combination of sampling units has the same chance of being in the sample. The auditor has to be sure that the sample being selected is representative of the population from which it is drawn.

Random sampling typically involves the following steps:

▶ Relating identifying numbers (or letters) to sampling units in the population

▶ Deriving a random sample from the population with the aid of a random number table or a random number generator computer program

The sampling unit may be in physical terms. Examples of physical identifiers are check number, invoice number, page number, and warehouse row and bin number.

Random sampling may be used for nonstatistical and statistical applications.

Systematic sampling technique

Systematic sampling consists of sequencing all items of the population. Sampling units are put in order (e.g., numerical). Audit software exist having routines for systematic sampling. The auditor then divides the population into *n* intervals of equal size based on the number of sampling units that must be chosen for the sample *(n)*. He or she then chooses a sampling unit from each of the derived intervals. The selection interval can be determined by dividing the population size *(N)* by the required sample size *(n)*.

Example 1

The auditor is examining 1,000 sales invoices from a population of 20,000 invoices. One random starting point is employed. Each 20th invoice is chosen. In order that 1,000 invoices are selected, the auditor moves up or down from the random starting point. If a random starting point of invoice number 100 is selected, invoice number 80 (100 — 20) and 60 (100 — 40) are included in the sample, as well as every 20th invoice number after 100 (i.e., 120, 140, 160, and so on). If the auditor selected 10 random starting points, 100 invoices (1000/10) would be selected for audit. Thus, the auditor would select every 200th invoice number (20,000/100) before and after each random beginning point.

Example 2

The population is 10,000 units and the sample size is 1,000 units. The auditor selects a random starting point between one and the sampling interval of 10 (10,000/1,000). This forces the auditor to choose the first sampling unit from the first interval. After including the random start unit as part of the sample, the accountant then sequentially selects every 10th item of the population. Typically, this approach results in a true random sample. Note that if a cyclical pattern in the population exists that coincides with the selection interval, a bias may result, i.e., if every 10th sampling unit or multiple of 10 happens to be a departmental manager, then based on the random start, the sample derived may yield either all departmental managers or none. However, the possibility of introducing a bias into the sample as a result of a cyclical pattern in the population would be minimized by picking multiple starting points in the selection process. But if multiple starting points are chosen, then the sampling interval that was previously selected must be multiplied by the number of random starts so that the required sample size is unchanged.

When there is no numerical sequence to a population, the auditor will find it easier to use a systematic random sample rather than a pure random sample. If documents, records, or transactions are unnumbered, there is no need with systematic sampling to number them physically. If random number table selection was involved, the drawback would be to require numbering. With systematic sampling, the auditor uses the sampling interval as the basis for selecting the document to examine.

Systematic sampling may be employed for both statistical and nonstatistical sampling.

Attribute sampling

An attribute is defined as a characteristic that a component of the population has or does not have. For instance, a customer's account is either past due or not. Authorization to pay a vendor has either been given or not.

Attribute sampling tests binary, yes/no, or error/nonerror questions. In attribute sampling, an estimate is made of the proportion of the population that contains a particular characteristic. It can apply to a random sample of physical units or to a systematic sample that approximates a random sample. A sample item possesses or does not possess the specific characteristic. No consideration is given to the magnitude of the characteristic. Based on the sample result, it is found if the true occurrence rate in the population is not greater than a specified percentage expressed at a given reliability level. The auditor may test for several different attributes in a sample.

Attribute sampling is based on a binomial distribution. An estimation may be made of the probable occurrence rates of particular characteristics in a population where each characteristic has two mutually exclusive outcomes. Software for attribute sampling purposes are available from time sharing vendors.

An application of attribute sampling is the auditor's substantiation of breakdown of control procedures. Examples are the measurement of the degree of breakdown of control procedures related to cash disbursements, cash receipts, sales, payroll, and the extent of incorrect entries and incorrect postings.

Attribute sampling of physical units cannot be employed to estimate the total of a variable characteristic (e.g., values).

In determining the initial size of an attribute sample, the initial size for an attribute sample is based on sampling risk in the form of the risk of assessing control risk too low (the complement of the confidence level for attribute sampling), the tolerable deviation rate, and the expected population deviation rate. The auditor should select an acceptable risk level. In practical terms, auditors select either a 5% or 10% risk because these levels will furnish the auditor with a 95% or 90% confidence, respectively, that the sample is representative of the population. The lower the risk the auditor selects, the greater will be the sample size.

A tolerable deviation rate will have to be selected. It is the maximum rate of deviation the auditor is willing to tolerate and still be able to rely on the control. The tolerable rate depends on professional judgment and the extent of reliance placed on the control or procedure. The following guidelines exist:

DEGREE OF RELIANCE	TOLERABLE RATE
Little	11—20%
Moderate	6—12%
Substantial	2—7%

An evaluation should be made of the anticipated deviation rate which may be based on deviations in prior years taking into account corrective changes in the current year.
The actual deviation rate in the sample equals:

$$\frac{\text{Number of Deviations}}{\text{Sample Size}}$$

The auditor should ascertain whether the deviations are due to errors (unintentional) or irregularities (intentional). When the sample deviation is in excess of the tolerable rate, no reliance may be placed on the control.

In examining the population, the population should be complete so that representative testing is possible. For instance, in testing purchase transactions, unpaid as well as paid invoices should be included.

The auditor should define the period covered by the examination. If interim testing is involved, the period after testing to the end of the year should be reviewed. Consideration should be given to the nature and amount of transactions and balances, and the length of the remaining period. The working papers should contain definitions of attributes and occurrences.

Attribute sampling is helpful in tests of controls. An example is evaluating the appropriateness of accounting controls through transaction testing.

Tables are referred to in determining sample size given the risk of over-reliance, tolerable occurrence rate, and anticipated occurrence rate.

Example 3

In ascertaining if the credit department is performing well, Bill Lund, CPA uses attribute sampling in examining sales orders through tests of controls. Lund determines that: (1) the deviation condition is the lack of the credit manager's initials on a sales order, (2) the population is comprised of the duplicate sales orders for the whole year, (3) the sampling unit is the sales order, (4) random number selection is used, (5) a 5% risk of assessing control risk too low will be used, (6) the tolerable rate of deviation is 6%, and (7) the anticipated population deviation rate is 2%.

Using Table 1, 127 is the sample size. Lund uses a random number table (Table 5) to select the sample. Because the population is comprised of sales orders numbered 1 to 500, Lund decides to use the first three digits of items selected from the random number table. With a blind start at column 5, row 6, Lund selects the following sales orders: 277, 188, 174, 496, 482, 312, and so on.

After carrying out the sampling plan, Lund discovers that four sales orders are missing the credit manager's signature (apparently an error on the part of the credit manager). The sample deviation rate is thus 4/127 or 3.1%. The upper occurrence limit, determined by referring to Table 3 is 7.2. In evaluating the results, 125 is used for the sample size for conservative reasons. Because the upper occurrence limit exceeds the tolerable rate of 6%, Lund rejects the control and attempts to identify a compensating control for additional testing.

Discovery sampling

Discovery sampling is used in a search for critical deviations such as for fraud and irregularities. This sampling technique may be employed when the auditor wants to determine if an acceptable irregularity rate in the population has been exceeded. If the rate is not excessive, no additional audit testing is required. If it is exceeded, alternative audit procedures are necessary. An attribute estimate may also be required. In discovery sampling, there is a minimum sample size that would include at least one irregularity if the population errors were greater than a given rate. Hence, if one irregularity is found in the sample, the test is resolved. Because discovery sampling is based on a minimum sample size to uncover only one irregularity, the sample size has to be increased in the event a useful attribute estimate is needed, such as the real irregularity rate in the population.

In using discovery sampling, a determination has to be made regarding population size, minimum unacceptable error rate, and confidence level. Sample size is determined from a sampling table. In the event that none of the random samples show an irregularity, it is concluded that the actual irregularity rate is less than the minimum unacceptable irregularity rate at the desired confidence level. Typically, the technique is used to spot groups of documents needing thorough testing.

Example 4

The auditor suspects fraud and wants to determine if any such fraud exists. The auditor is examining vouchers for proper authorization. Cost = benefit makes it not practical for the auditor to look at all vouchers. Discovery sampling can be used to obtain a 90% confidence level that the absence of proper authorization is less than 1%. According to the table, for 2,000 voucher items, a random sample size of 220 is needed. If fraud does not exist in the sample, we can conclude that the population contains less than 1% fraud. In the event a single fraudulent situation is found, the auditor stops sampling and examines all vouchers.

Multistage sampling

Multistage sampling consists of sampling at multilevels where an estimate of the total dollars of the population that is in groups over a wide area is required. For example, if an estimate of the total dollar value of inventory of a chain store or supermarket with widely distributed outlets is required, the multistage techniques would be appropriate. Selections at any level may be accomplished using alternative sampling methods (e.g., random, stratified, systematic).

Multistage sampling will necessitate a larger sample size and more sophisticated evaluation formulas than is the case with simple or stratified sampling methods.

Table 1: 5 Percent Risk of control risk too low

Statistical Sample Sizes for Tests of Controls (For Large Populations)

Expected Population Deviation Rate	Tolerable Occurrence Rate								
	2%	3%	4%	5%	6%	7%	8%	9%	10%
0.00%	129	99	74	59	49	42	36	32	29
.50	*	157	117	93	78	66	58	51	46
1.00	*	*	156	93	78	66	58	51	46
1.50	*	*	192	124	103	66	58	51	46
2.00	*	*	*	181	127	88	77	68	46
2.50	*	*	*	*	150	109	77	68	61
3.00	*	*	*	*	195	129	95	84	61
4.00	*	*	*	*	*	*	146	100	89
5.00	*	*	*	*	*	*	*	158	116
6.00	*	*	*	*	*	*	*	*	179

Table 2: 10 Percent Risk of Assessing Control Risk Too Low

Expected Population Deviation Rate	Tolerable Occurrence Rate								
	2%	3%	4%	5%	6%	7%	8%	9%	10%
0.00%	114	76	57	45	38	32	28	25	22
.50	194	129	96	77	64	55	48	42	38
1.00	*	176	96	77	64	55	48	42	38
1.50	*	*	132	105	64	55	48	42	38
2.00	*	*	198	132	88	75	48	42	38
2.50	*	*	*	158	110	75	65	58	38
3.00	*	*	*	*	132	94	65	58	52
4.00	*	*	*	*	*	149	98	73	65
5.00	*	*	*	*	*	*	160	115	78
6.00	*	*	*	*	*	*	*	182	116

*Sample size is too large to be cost effective for most audit applications.

Table 3: 5 Percent Risk of Asssessing Control Risk Too Low

Statistical Sample Results Evaluation Table for Test of Controls
Upper Occurrence Limit (for large populations)

Sample Size	Actual Number of Occurrences Found								
	0	1	2	3	4	5	6	7	8
25	11.3	17.6	*	*	*	*	*	*	*
30	9.5	14.9	19.5	*	*	*	*	*	*
35	8.2	12.9	16.9	*	*	*	*	*	*
40	7.2	11.3	14.9	18.3	*	*	*	*	*
45	6.4	10.1	13.3	16.3	19.2	*	*	*	*
50	5.8	9.1	12.1	14.8	17.4	19.9	*	*	*
55	5.3	8.3	11.0	13.5	15.9	18.1	*	*	*
60	4.9	7.7	10.1	12.4	14.6	16.7	18.8	*	*
65	4.5	7.1	9.4	11.5	13.5	15.5	17.4	19.3	*
70	4.2	6.6	8.7	10.7	12.6	14.4	16.2	18.0	19.7
75	3.9	6.2	8.2	10.0	11.8	13.5	15.2	16.9	18.4
80	3.7	5.8	7.7	9.4	11.1	12.7	14.3	15.8	17.3
90	3.3	5.2	6.8	8.4	9.9	11.3	12.7	14.1	15.5
100	3.0	4.7	6.2	7.6	8.9	10.2	11.5	12.7	14.0
125	2.4	3.7	4.9	6.1	7.2	8.2	9.3	10.3	11.3
150	2.0	3.1	4.1	5.1	6.0	6.9	7.7	8.6	9.4
200	1.5	2.3	3.1	3.8	4.5	5.2	5.8	6.5	7.1

Variables sampling

Variables sampling applies to dollar values or other quantities in contrast with the binary proposition tested by attribute sampling. It is used for *substantive testing*, which attempts to provide evidence about whether an account balance is materially misstated.

Variables sampling is comprised of a family of three statistical techniques (mean per unit approach, difference sampling, and ratio sampling) which use normal distribution theory and are concerned with ascertaining whether the total dollar values of account balances are properly stated. The method estimates the statistical range within which the true account balance being tested falls. It requires an estimate of population variability (population standard deviation) and necessitates the use of a computer.

It is an approach to predict the value of a particular variable in the population. Audit-related variables are usually the total population or the arithmetic mean. For example, an auditor may estimate the cost of a group of inventory components. The per-item cost is determined. Finally, there is a statistical derivation of the plus-or-minus range of the total inventory value under audit.

Table 4: 10 Percent risk of assessing control risk too low

Sample Size	Actual Number of Occurrences Found								
	0	1	2	3	4	5	6	7	8
20	10.9	18.1	*	*	*	*	*	*	*
25	8.8	14.7	19.9	*	*	*	*	*	*
30	7.4	12.4	16.8	*	*	*	*	*	*
35	6.4	10.7	14.5	18.1	*	*	*	*	*
40	5.6	9.4	12.8	15.9	19.0	*	*	*	*
45	5.0	8.4	11.4	14.2	17.0	19.6	*	*	*
50	4.5	7.6	10.3	12.9	15.4	17.8	*	*	*
55	4.1	6.9	9.4	11.7	14.0	16.2	18.4	*	*
60	3.8	6.3	8.6	10.8	12.9	14.9	15.9	18.8	*
70	3.2	5.4	7.4	9.3	11.1	12.8	14.6	16.2	17.9
80	2.8	4.8	6.5	8.3	9.7	11.3	12.8	14.3	15.7
90	2.5	4.3	5.8	7.3	8.7	10.1	11.4	12.7	14.0
100	2.3	3.8	5.2	6.6	7.8	9.1	10.3	11.5	12.7
120	1.9	3.2	4.4	5.5	6.6	7.6	8.6	9.6	10.6
160	1.4	2.4	3.3	4.1	4.9	5.7	6.5	7.2	8.0
200	1.1	1.9	2.6	3.3	4.0	4.6	5.2	5.8	6.4

*over 20%

Stratified sampling

When using stratified sampling, the auditor segregates the population into homogeneous subgroups (strata) according to a common characteristic (such as the stratification of total credit sales into open account sales and credit card sales). The auditor then samples each stratum. The sample results should be appraised separately and combined to provide an estimate of the population characteristics. Homogeneity is enhanced when very high- or low- value items are segregated into individual strata. Homogeneity in the population improves the efficiency of the sample. Thus, usually fewer items have to be examined to appraise several strata separately than to evaluate the whole population. Stratification benefits the sampling process and enhances auditor ability to relate sample selection to the materiality and turnover of items. The type of audit procedures applied to each stratum may vary based on individual circumstances and the nature of the environment. An application of stratified sampling is when total inventory (population) is broken down into major groups based on dollar balances for testing purposes. An illustration follows:

STRATUM	METHOD OF SELECTION USED
1. All inventory items of $50,000 or more	100% tested
2. All other inventory items under $50,000	Random number table selection

Judgement (nonstatistical) sampling

Nonstatistical sampling is when an auditor uses his or her prior experience and knowledge to compute the number of sampling units and specific items to be studied from the population. The sample takes into account the nature of the business and unique characteristics that may exist. The auditor must be objective in carrying out the sample and perform detailed analysis to assure the sampled units are correct. This approach may be advisable when a particular area of the population is being carefully examined or immediate results and feedback are needed. This technique is used primarily when the audit population consists of either a small number of high-dollar-value items or items with an immaterial aggregate cost. For example, this approach may be used in selecting twenty additions to property and equipment, worth $200,000, for vouching when total additions consist of 40 items aggregating $250,000.

Note: A nonstatistical sample does not involve random selection. There is no computation made of sampling error, precision, or confidence level. Thus, there is an absence of statistical techniques and conclusions.

In using nonstatistical sampling, the auditor considers the same factors in determining sample size and in evaluating sample results as in statistical sampling. The difference is that in nonstatistical sampling, the auditor does not quantify or explicitly enumerate values for these factors. In statistical sampling, however, they are explicitly quantified. That is, in nonstatistical sampling, the auditor determines the sample size, selects a sample, and evaluates the sample results entirely on the basis of subjective criteria and his or her own experience, i.e., judgment. In addition, it is important to note that a properly designed nonstatistical sample may be just as effective as a statistical sample.

Table 5: Random Number Table

Line	(1)	(2)	(3)	(4)	(5)	(6)	(7)	(8)	(9)	(10)	(11)	(12)	(13)	(14)
1	10480	15011	01536	02011	81647	91646	69179	14194	62590	36207	20969	99570	91291	90700
2	22368	46573	25595	85393	30995	89198	27982	53402	93965	34095	52666	19174	39615	99505
3	24130	48360	22527	97265	76393	64809	15179	24830	49340	32081	30680	19655	63348	58629
4	42167	93093	06243	61650	07856	16376	39440	53537	71341	57004	00849	74917	97758	16379
5	37570	39975	81837	16656	06121	91782	60468	81305	49684	60672	14110	06927	01263	34613
6	77921	06907	11008	42751	27756	53498	18602	70659	90655	15053	21916	81825	44394	42880
7	99562	72905	56420	69994	98872	31016	71194	18738	44013	48840	63213	21069	19634	12952
8	96301	91977	05463	07972	18876	20922	94595	56869	69014	60045	18425	84903	42508	32307
9	89579	14342	63661	10281	17453	18103	57740	84378	25331	12566	58678	44947	05585	56941
10	85475	36857	53342	53988	53060	59533	38867	62300	08158	17983	16439	11458	18593	64952
11	28918	69578	88231	33276	70997	79936	56865	05859	90106	31595	01547	85590	91610	78188
12	63553	40961	48235	03427	49626	69445	18663	72695	52180	20847	12234	90511	33703	90332
13	09429	93969	52636	92737	88974	33488	36320	17617	30015	08272	84115	27156	30613	74952
14	10365	61129	87529	85689	48237	52267	67689	93394	01511	26358	85104	20285	29975	89868
15	07119	97336	71048	08178	77233	13916	47564	81056	97735	85977	29372	74461	28551	90707
16	51085	12765	51821	51259	77452	16308	60756	92144	49442	53900	70960	63990	75601	40719
17	02368	21382	52404	60268	89368	19885	55322	44819	01188	63255	64835	44919	05944	55157
18	01011	54092	33362	94904	31273	04146	18594	29852	71585	85030	51132	01915	92747	64951
19	52162	53916	46369	58586	23216	14513	83149	98736	23495	64350	94738	17752	35156	35749
20	07056	97628	33787	09998	42698	06691	76988	13602	51851	46104	88916	19509	25625	58104
21	48663	91245	85828	14346	09172	30168	90229	04734	59193	22178	30421	61666	99904	32812
22	54164	58492	22421	74103	47070	25306	76468	26384	58151	06646	21524	15227	96909	44592
23	32639	32363	05597	24200	13363	38005	94342	28728	35806	06912	17012	64161	18296	22851

Fraud Prevention, Fraud Detection, and Forensic Accounting

Virtually every entity suffers from fraud, though they may not know it. Fraud is a growing problem, despite attempts to control it, costing entities an average of 6% of their revenues. Especially in the heels of the Enron debacle, a series of corporate scandals, and terrorism, the ranks of specialized forensic accountants and fraud examiners who sniff out financial shenanigans by practicing a mix of accounting, law, technology, ethics, and criminology are growing. Since its founding in 1988, the Association of Certified Fraud Examiner (ACFE) has swelled to 25,000 members in 105 countries. And all of the Big Four accounting firms have recently formed forensic-accounting and fraud-detection units.

Fraud prevention

How vulnerable is your company to fraud? Do you have adequate controls in place to prevent it? Fraud can be a catastrophic risk. If you don't proactively identify and manage your fraud risks, they could put you out of business almost overnight. Even if you survive a major fraud, it can damage your reputation so badly that you can no longer succeed independently. It could pinpoint opportunities to save you a lot of money. Fraud is an expensive drain on an entity's financial resources. In today's globally competitive environment, no one can afford to throw away the 6% of revenues that represents the largely hidden cost of fraud. Those businesses that have identified their most significant fraud costs (such as insurance and credit card companies) have made great strides in attacking and reducing those costs. If an entity isn't identifying and tackling its fraud costs, it is vulnerable to competitors who lower their costs by doing so. Fraud is now a common risk that shouldn't be ignored. The incidence of fraud is now so common that its occurrence is no longer remarkable, only its scale. Any entity that fails to protect itself appropriately from fraud should expect to become a victim of fraud, or rather, should expect to discover that it is a victim of fraud.

The Association of Certified Fraud Examiner (ACFE) has developed a *Fraud Prevention Check-Up System*. It is a simple yet powerful test of your company's fraud health. Test fraud prevention processes designed to help you identify major gaps and fix them before it is too late. It is an affordable, easy-to-use method to identify gaps in your company's fraud prevention process. In fact, most companies score poorly on their initial Fraud Prevention Check-Up because they don't have appropriate anti-fraud controls in place. By identifying risks early, they have a chance to fix the problem before becoming a victim of a major fraud.

Strong fraud prevention processes bolster the confidence investors, regulators, audit committee members and the general public have in the integrity of your company's reports, which will help you attract and retain capital.

▶ The number of points available is given at the bottom of each question. You can award zero points if your entity has not implemented the recommended processes for that area. You can give the maximum number of points if you have implemented those processes and have had them tested in the past year and found them to be operating effectively. *Award no more than half the available points if the recommended process is in place but has not been tested in the past year.*

▶ The purpose of the checkup is to identify major gaps in your fraud prevention processes, as indicated by low point scores in particular areas. Even if you score 80 points out of 100, the missing 20 could be crucial fraud prevention measures that leave you exposed to major fraud. So there is no passing grade other than 100 points.

The ACFE Fraud Prevention Checkup

	RESULTS
Entity: Date of Checkup:	
1. **Fraud risk oversight** To what extent has the entity established a process for oversight of fraud risks by the board of directors or others charged with governance (e.g., an audit committee)? Score: From 0 (process not in place) to 20 points (process fully implemented, tested within the past year and working effectively).	
2. **Fraud risk ownership** To what extent has the entity created "ownership" of fraud risks by identifying a member of senior management as having responsibility for managing all fraud risks within the entity and by explicitly communicating to business unit managers that they are responsible for managing fraud risks within their part of the entity? Score: From 0 (process not in place) to 10 points (process fully implemented, tested within the past year and working effectively).	
3. **Fraud risk assessment** To what extent has the entity implemented an ongoing process for regular identification of the significant fraud risks to which the entity is exposed? Score: From 0 (process not in place) to 10 points (process fully implemented, tested within the past year and working effectively).	

	RESULTS
4. **Fraud risk tolerance and risk management policy** To what extent has the entity identified and had approved by the board of directors its tolerance for different types of fraud risks? For example, some fraud risks may constitute a tolerable cost of doing business, while others may pose a catastrophic risk of financial or reputational damage to the entity. The entity will likely have a different tolerance for these risks. To what extent has the entity identified and had approved by the board of directors a policy on how the entity will manage its fraud risks? Such a policy should identify the risk owner responsible for managing fraud risks, what risks will be rejected (e.g., by declining certain business opportunities), what risks will be transferred to others through insurance or by contract, and what steps will be taken to manage the fraud risks that are retained. Score: From 0 (processes not in place) to 10 points (processes fully implemented, tested within the past year and working effectively).	

	RESULTS
5. Process level anti-fraud controls/ re-engineering To what extent has the entity implemented measures, where possible, to eliminate or reduce through process re-engineering each of the significant fraud risks identified in its risk assessment? Basic controls include segregation of duties relating to authorization, custody of assets and recording or reporting of transactions. In some cases it may be more cost-effective to re-engineer business processes to reduce fraud risks rather than layer on additional controls over existing processes. For example, some fraud risks relating to receipt of funds can be eliminated or greatly reduced by centralizing that function or outsourcing it to a bank's lockbox processing facility, where stronger controls can be more affordable. To what extent has the entity implemented measures at the process level designed to prevent, deter and detect each of the significant fraud risks identified in its risk assessment? For example, the risk of sales representatives falsifying sales to earn sales commissions can be reduced through effective monitoring by their sales manager, with approval required for sales above a certain threshold. Score: From 0 (processes not in place) to 10 points (processes fully implemented, tested within the past year and working effectively).	

		RESULTS
6.	**Environment level anti-fraud controls**	

6. Environment level anti-fraud controls

Major frauds usually involve senior members of management who are able to override process-level controls through their high level of authority. Preventing major frauds therefore requires a very strong emphasis on creating a workplace environment that promotes ethical behavior, deters wrongdoing and encourages all employees to communicate any known or suspected wrongdoing to the appropriate person. Senior managers may be unable to perpetrate certain fraud schemes if employees decline to aid and abet them in committing a crime. Although "soft" controls to promote appropriate workplace behavior are more difficult to implement and evaluate than traditional "hard" controls, they appear to be the best defense against fraud involving senior management.

To what extent has the entity implemented a process to promote ethical behavior, deter wrongdoing and facilitate two-way communication on difficult issues? Such a process typically includes:

–   Having a senior member of management who is responsible for the entity's processes to promote ethical behavior, deter wrongdoing and communicate appropriately on difficult issues. In large public companies, this may be a full-time position as ethics officer or compliance officer. In smaller companies, this will be an additional responsibility held by an existing member of management.

	RESULTS
– A code of conduct for employees at all levels, based on the entity's core values, which gives clear guidance on what behavior and actions are permitted and which ones are prohibited. The code should identify how employees should seek additional advice when faced with uncertain ethical decisions and how they should communicate concerns about known or potential wrongdoing affecting the entity. – Training for all personnel upon hiring and regularly thereafter concerning the code of conduct, seeking advice and communicating potential wrongdoing.	

	RESULTS
– Communication systems to enable employees to seek advice where necessary prior to making difficult ethical decisions and to express concern about known or potential wrongdoing affecting the entity. Advice systems may include an ethics or compliance telephone help line or e- mail to an ethics or compliance office/officer. The same or similar systems may be used to enable employees (and sometimes vendors, customers and others) to communicate concerns about known or potential wrongdoing affecting the entity. Provision should be made to enable such communications to be made anonymously, though strenuous efforts should be made to create an environment in which callers feel sufficiently confident to express their concerns openly. Open communication makes it easier for the entity to resolve the issues raised, but protecting callers from retribution is an important concern.	

	RESULTS
– A process for promptly investigating where appropriate and resolving expressions of concern regarding known or potential wrongdoing, then communicating the resolution to those who expressed the concern. The entity should have a plan that sets out what actions will be taken and by whom to investigate and resolve different types of concerns. Some issues will be best addressed by human resources personnel, some by general counsel, some by internal auditors and some may require investigation by fraud specialists. Having a pre-arranged plan will greatly speed and ease the response and will ensure appropriate persons are notified where significant potential issues are involved (e.g., legal counsel, board of directors, audit committee, independent auditors, regulators, etc.) – Monitoring of compliance with the code of conduct and participation in the related training. Monitoring may include requiring at least annual confirmation of compliance and auditing of such confirmations to test their completeness and accuracy.	

	RESULTS
– Regular measurement of the extent to which the entity's ethics/ compliance and fraud prevention goals are being achieved. Such measurement typically includes surveys of a statistically meaningful sample of employees. Surveys of employees' attitudes towards the entity's ethics/compliance activities and the extent to which employees believe management acts in accordance with the code of conduct provide invaluable insight into how well those items are functioning. – Incorporation of ethics/compliance and fraud prevention goals into the performance measures against which managers are evaluated and which are used to determine performance related compensation. Score: From 0 (process not in place) to 30 points (process fully implemented, tested within the past year and working effectively).	

	RESULTS
7. Proactive fraud detection To what extent has the entity established a process to detect, investigate and resolve potentially significant fraud? Such a process should typically include proactive fraud detection tests that are specifically designed to detect the significant potential frauds identified in the entity's fraud risk assessment. Other measures can include audit "hooks" embedded in the entity's transaction processing systems that can flag suspicious transactions for investigation and/or approval prior to completion of processing. Leading edge fraud detection methods include computerized e-mail monitoring (where legally permitted) to identify use of certain phrases that might indicate planned or ongoing wrongdoing. Score: From 0 (process not in place) to 10 points (process fully implemented, tested within the past year and working effectively). TOTAL SCORE (Out of a possible 100 points):	

	RESULTS
Interpreting the Entity's Score A brief fraud prevention checkup provides a broad idea of the entity's performance with respect to fraud prevention. The scoring necessarily involves broad judgments, while more extensive evaluations would have greater measurement data to draw upon. Therefore the important information to take from the checkup is the identification of particular areas for improvement in the entity's fraud prevention processes. The precise numerical score is less important and is only presented to help communicate an overall impression. The desirable score for an entity of any size is 100 points, since the recommended processes are scalable to the size of the entity. Most entities should expect to fall significantly short of 100 points in an initial fraud prevention checkup. That is not currently considered to be a material weakness in internal controls that represents a reportable condition under securities regulations. However, significant gaps in fraud prevention measures should be closed promptly in order to reduce fraud losses and reduce the risk of future disaster	

Source: Association of Certified Fraud Examiners
(www.CFEnet.com).

Forensic accounting and auditing

Forensic accounting is a science (i.e., a department of systemized knowledge) dealing with the application of accounting facts gathered through auditing methods and procedures to resolve legal problems. Forensic accounting is much different from traditional auditing. The main purpose of a traditional audit is to examine the financial statements of an organization and express an opinion on the fairness of the financial statements. In other words, auditors give an opinion whether the financial statements have been prepared in accordance with generally accepted accounting principles. Auditors employ limited procedures and use extensive testing and sampling techniques.

Audits are performed by independent accountants and are not conducted with a view to present the evidence in a judicial forum. An audit is not an investigation; its main objective is not to uncover fraud.

Forensic accounting, on the other hand, is for investigation of an allegation with the assumption that the forensic accountant will have to present the evidence in a judicial forum. A forensic accountant often employs specialists in other areas as part of a team to gather evidence. In order to present the evidence in court, there must be absolute assurance; thus testing and sampling methods are usually not employed as part of the evidence gathering procedures. The scope of the investigation is limited because it is determined by the client.

Forensic accounting, therefore, is a specialty requiring the integration of investigative, accounting, and auditing skills. The forensic accountant looks at documents and financial and other data in a critical manner in order to draw conclusions and to calculate values, and to identify irregular patterns and/or suspicious transactions. A forensic accountant understands the fraud risk areas and has extensive fraud knowledge. A forensic accountant does not merely look at the numbers but rather, looks *behind* the numbers.

One can extend this definition to say that forensic accounting is a discipline consisting of two areas of specialization; namely, litigation support specialists and investigation or fraud accountants. Litigation support specialists concern themselves with business valuation, testimony as expert witnesses, future earnings' evaluation, and income and expense analysis. On the other hand, *fraud accountants* apply their skills to investigate areas of alleged criminal misconduct in order to support or dispel damages. These fields overlap—a forensic accountant may do litigation support work on one engagement and act as a fraud accountant on another. Both of these engagements could result in expert testimony by the forensic accountant. Thus, forensic accounting can be defined in a more generic way: It is merely a discipline where auditing, accounting, and investigative skills are used to assist in disputes involving financial issues and data, and where there is suspicion or allegation of fraud. The expertise of the forensic accountant may be used to support a plaintiff who is trying to establish a claim, or to support a defendant in order to minimize the impact of a claim against him or her. Usually such investigations involve litigation; sometimes, however, such disputes are settled by negotiation. In either case, persuasive and authoritative evidence resulting from the financial and investigative skills of the forensic accountant is imperative. Therefore, the forensic accountant must be a good businessperson and be aware of statutory law, common law, and the laws of evidence and procedure.

Usually the forensic accountant's findings are based on facts, not opinions. Facts can be investigated, and the forensic accountant can prepare a definitive report on these facts. Nevertheless, there are situations where the forensic accountant may rely on professional judgment and present findings using an opinion-type report. Needless to say, the reports based on facts usually do not present problems in court cases because they are supported by underlying documentation. Opinion reports, on the other hand, are subjective and require the forensic accountant to demonstrate competency and to provide adequate logic for the stated opinion.

Two points are often overlooked when one is involved in a case as a forensic accountant; namely, (1) the other side usually employs a forensic accountant as well; and (2) the credibility of a forensic accountant is extremely important. Thus the forensic accountant must have high professional standards and ethics.

Forensic accounting and fraud examination

Again, forensic accounting is an accounting specialty that integrates accounting, auditing, and investigative skills in order to support or resolve allegations of fraud. Forensic Accounting encompasses both litigation support (expert witness testimony, presentation of supporting documents showing fraud, etc.) and investigative accounting.

The difference between a "normal" accountant and a forensic accountant is that the latter seeks a level of evidentiary detail and analytical precision, which will be sustainable with legal scrutiny or review.

Forensic Accounting focuses on both the evidence of economic transactions and reporting, and the legal framework that allows such evidence to be suitable for establishing accountability and/or valuation. Forensic Accounting engagements include transaction reconstruction; bankruptcy; family law issues; asset identification and valuation; fraud examination/detection; and many other issues.

Auditing is performed either by an employee (internal audit) or by an outside accounting firm (external audit). Internal audits examine *operational evidence* to ensure that the prescribed company operating procedures have been followed. External audits examine the assets and records of a company, leading to the expression of a professional opinion by the outside CPA, which gives credibility to the financial reports presented by the company. A key component of an audit is the review of internal control weaknesses. Fraud examination differs from auditing as shown in Exhibit 1:

Exhibit 1: Auditing vs. Fraud Examination

ISSUE	AUDITING	FRAUD EXAMINATION
Timing	**Recurring** Audits are conducted on a regular, recurring basis.	**Nonrecurring** Fraud examinations are nonrecurring. They are conducted only with sufficient predication.
Scope	**General** The scope of the audit is an examination of financial data.	**Specific** The fraud examination is conducted to resolve specific allegations.
Objective	**Opinion** An audit is generally conducted for the purpose of expressing an opinion on the financial statements or related information.	**Affix blame** The fraud examination's goal is to determine whether fraud has occurred or is occurring and to determine who is responsible.
Relationship	**Nonadversarial** The audit process is nonadversarial in nature.	**Adversarial** Fraud examinations, because they involve efforts to affix blame, are adversarial in nature.
Methodology	**Audit techniques** Audits are conducted by examining financial data and obtaining corroborating evidence.	**Fraud examination techniques** Fraud examinations are conducted by (1) document examination; (2) review of outside data such as public records; and (3) interviews.
Standard	**Professional skepticism** Auditors are required to approach audits with professional skepticism.	**Proof** Fraud examiners approach the resolution of a fraud by attempting to establish sufficient proof to support or refute a fraud allegation.

Source: Fraud Examiners Manual, Association of Certified Fraud Examiners, 2005.

Why is forensic accounting necessary?

Business and criminal activities have become so complex that lawyers and criminal investigators often do not have the expertise necessary to discharge their responsibilities. This fact plus the marked increase in white-collar crime, marital and business disputes, and other claims have created the need for the new industry of forensic accounting. Although this specialty is not limited to fraud issues, nevertheless, the reality of forensic accounting is that most of the work does involve fraud investigations. In the case of fraud, the work of a forensic accounting team is crucial, as the survival of the business may rest on the outcome. Good business people must realize that fraud is a permanent risk in any and all businesses. Thus company leaders must devise ways to prevent fraud rather than trying to manage the consequences of fraud. The instances of fraud have increased because of lack of government commitment, more sophisticated criminals, inefficiency of the judicial system, more complex technology, lack of adequate penalties and deterrents, and "old fashioned" greed and arrogance. Studies have shown that fraud will continue to increase. Currently, about 75% of fraud results from employees; other sources of fraud include customers, management, suppliers, and service providers. In addition, about 55% of fraud is discovered as a result of strong internal controls. Other methods of discovery include whistle blowers, customers, internal auditors, and by accident or formal investigation.

In today's business environment where economic pressures, insufficient emphasis on prevention and protection and an increased level of sophistication among criminals exist, the incidents of business fraud are on the rise.

Every business is susceptible to fraud no matter their size.

Fraud can occur because of:

▶ Poor Internal Controls
▶ Management Overrides of Internal Controls
▶ Collusion Between Employees & Third Parties
▶ Collusion Between Employees or Management
▶ Lack of Control Over Management
▶ Poor or Non-existent Ethics Policy

Forensic accountants utilize a host of information databases and a local and national network of former FBI agents to support the expertise of CPAs. Their investigative orientation enables them to:

▶ Define the broad scope of their assignments.
▶ Structure and implement imaginative strategies.
▶ Develop sound internal controls.
▶ Develop a case for either civil or criminal disposition.

Most business owners associate business fraud with the misappropriations of cash. However, business fraud comes in many other forms including:

Average loss*

Medical Insurance Claims Fraud	$3,177,000
False Financial Statements	1,239,000
Credit Card Fraud	1,126,000
Check Fraud	624,000
Inventory Theft	346,000
Bid Rigging/price Fixing	342,000
False Invoices and Phantom Vendors	256,000
Diversion of Sales	180,000
Expense Account Abuse	141,000
Purchases for Personal Use	63,000
Conflict of Interest	38,000
Kickbacks	35,000
Payroll Fraud	26,000

Based on the results of a recent survey of 5,000 U.S. companies that have experienced fraud in their business.

Investigative services

▶ Due Diligence Research
▶ Forensic Accounting
▶ Embezzlements
▶ Vendor Fraud
▶ Internal Accounting Controls
▶ Litigation Support
▶ Pre-employment screening
▶ Public Record and Asset Research

Corporate services

▶ Fraud Prevention and Detection
▶ Fraud Audits
▶ Forensic Examinations
▶ Security Surveys
▶ Computer Fraud
▶ Economic Loss
▶ Information Loss

When does one employ a forensic accountant?

Clients retain forensic accountants when they are interested in either litigation support or investigations.

Litigation support

This is a situation where the forensic accountant is asked to give an opinion either on known facts or facts yet uncovered. The forensic accountant is an integral part of the legal team, helping to substantiate allegations, analyze facts, dispute claims, and develop motives. The amount of involvement and the point at which the forensic accountant gets involved varies from case to case. Sometimes the forensic accountant is called upon from the beginning of the case; other times the forensic accountant is summoned before the case is scheduled to go to court and after out-of-court settlements have failed. Thus, in litigation support, the forensic accountant assists in obtaining documentation to support or dispel a claim, to review documentation to give an assessment of the case to the legal team, and/or to identify areas where loss occurred. Moreover, the forensic accountant may be asked to get involved during the discovery stage to help formulate questions, and may be asked to review the opposing expert's witness report to give an evaluation of its strengths and weaknesses. During trial the forensic accountant may serve as an expert witness, help to provide questions for cross-examination, and assist with settlement discussions after the trial.

Investigations

Investigations most often involve fraud and are associated with criminal matters. Typically, an investigative accounting assignment would result from a client's suspicion that there is employee fraud. Other parties, such as regulatory agencies, police forces, and attorneys may retain a forensic accountant to investigate securities fraud, kickbacks, insurance fraud, money-laundering schemes, and asset search and analysis.

Where is a forensic accountant used?

A forensic accountant is used in a number of situations, including, but not limited to the following:

- ▶ *Business valuations:* A forensic accountant evaluates the current value of a business for various personal or legal matters.
- ▶ *Personal injury and fatal accident claims:* A forensic accountant may help to establish lost earnings (i.e., those earnings that the plaintiff would have

accrued except for the actions of the defendant) by gathering and analyzing a variety of information and then issuing a report based on the outcome of the analyses

▶ *Professional negligence:* A forensic accountant helps to determine if a breach of professional ethics or other standards of professional practice has occurred. (e.g., failure to apply generally accepted auditing standards by a CPA when performing an audit). In addition, the forensic accountant may help to quantify the loss.

▶ *Insurance claims evaluations:* A forensic accountant may prepare financial analyses for an insurance company of claims, business income losses, expenses, and disability, liability or workmen's compensation insurance losses.

▶ *Arbitration:* A forensic accountant is sometimes retained to assist with alternative dispute resolution (ADR) by acting as a mediator to allow individuals and businesses to resolve disputes in a timely manner with a minimum of disruption.

▶ *Partnership and corporation disputes:* A forensic accountant may be asked to help settle disputes between partners or shareholders. Detailed analyses are often necessary of many records spanning a number of years. Most of these disputes relate to compensation and benefit issues.

▶ *Civil and criminal actions concerning fraud and financial irregularities:*

These investigations are usually performed by the forensic accountant for police forces. A report is prepared to assist the prosecutor's office.

▶ *Fraud and white-collar crime investigations:* These types of investigations can be prepared on behalf of police forces as well or for private businesses. They usually result from such activities as purchasing/kickback schemes, computer fraud, labor fraud, and falsification of inventory. The investigation by the forensic accountant often involves fund tracing, asset identification, and recovery.

Litigation support consulting

In cases of litigation support consulting, the forensic accountant is asked to provide an opinion based on facts that can be known or as yet uncovered. In the case of the latter, the accountant may have to become an investigator of sorts, and on some occasions, prepare information as a model of how things should look if done correctly. Key areas of litigation support services include engagements in both professional liability claims as well as a variety of civil claims. Included in the professional liability claims category would be quantifying the impact of lost earnings from events such as construction delays, stolen trade secrets, insurance disputes, damage/loss estimates and malpractice claims. The category of civil claims includes business valuations, particularly in cases of divorce settlement, as well as employee theft and accident investigation.

Expert witness engagements

As a result of the increasingly litigious age in which we live, there is a growing need in the area of forensic accounting for expert witnesses. Whatever may be happening to the rest of the economy, litigation is booming, and so currently, is fraud. This creates an opportunity for accountants to act as experts. The accountant reviews the information concerning the matter at hand, and may or may not actually go to court. In fact, according to Justin de Lorenzo, the forensic accountant will probably spend less than five per cent of his time in the witness box because most disputes are settled out of court. However, when cases are settled out of court, a need is still prevalent for the expert witness.

The need for an expert witness generally arises when there is a dispute involving the area of accounting expertise. He may be called upon to perform economic fact finding, prepare a tax analysis, help take the deposition of the other party's expert witness, suggest avenues of inquiry, help interpret documentation, and assist in eliciting information from other witnesses.

Even though only a short amount of time is spent in the courtroom, it is the most critical because reputations are made and broken in the witness box. Therefore, it is imperative that the expert witness be more than just an accountant. The accountant must also be an educator and possess other necessary skills. Once in the courtroom, the accountant must treat the judge and jury as if they had no understanding of any accounting terms. For example, he/she needs to explain that net income does not necessarily equal cash in the bank. Also, several other hints for expert witness are to speak up and talk slowly. This enables the judge and jury to take notes, as well as simply understand what the witness is saying. He needs to keep statements short and simple, if possible, and avoid rambling. Also, the witness should avoid moving about too much as this gives a shifty impression. The expert witness should pause when needed and, if another look at a document is needed, request time to do so to ensure that precise information is being given. Some common sense approaches are not to argue with the lawyers or the judge while on the stand. The witness should look towards the jury when giving evidence, as well as attempt to build a rapport with the judge. Above all, the witness should try not to irritate the judge.

Entertaining the jury is also a positive attribute of a good expert witness because the jury's perception of his or her credibility could determine the client's case. The expert witness must know what to say, when to say it, and how to say it. He must know when to add humor and when to speak with authority. The key to becoming a good expert witness is the Three P's - Preparation! Preparation! Preparation!

Another grueling task of being an expert witness is that while he needs to actually do most of the research, he must definitely write the entire report. If the accountant delegates this work to someone else, he could be ripped apart under cross examination for not being totally familiar with the material. As a result of this, professional reputation and future opportunities could be destroyed.

Divorce business valuations

A forensic accountant may also play an important role in divorce settlements. If the husband and wife have ownership in a private company, a partnership or an unincorporated business, then the entity needs to be evaluated for financial breakdown. A forensic accountant may also be needed if either spouse is of significant financial worth. In this case, assets may need to be located, valued and allocated between the two parties.

The forensic accountant does not need to know all the logistics of matrimonial law, although he or she should be somewhat familiar with recent cases on the matter at hand. Specifically, the accountant should be versed in S23 and S25, which are of the Matrimonial Causes Act of 1973. S23 and S25 both deal with the financial aspects of divorce settlements and how they impact the decisions of the courts.

When analyzing a company, the accountant must focus on the earnings capability of the business as the company may not be financially stable at the time of the proceedings. To accomplish this, the accountant must determine possible borrowings and distributable future cash flows to assist the court in determining the proper settlement. Without this informed determination, each party would be presenting a strictly arbitrary figure.

Specifically, the objective of a divorce-related business valuation is to establish a realistic value, often with limited information, that is both consistent with the client's goal and defendable under cross examination in the courtroom. The forensic accountant must first understand that due to the controversial matter at hand, all available financial data may not be turned over for evaluation. That data which is received may be a misrepresentation of the true financial picture. To compensate for this possibility, the accountant must delve deeper into the presented financial information for areas of concern that may be hidden from the face value of the balance sheets and earnings statements.

On the balance sheets, key areas of concern for the forensic accountant include the possibility of hidden assets and liabilities. Specific examples of these include the following: the existence of fully depreciated equipment; unrecorded leases made under favorable conditions; misstated inventories; ownership of franchise and royalties rights; underfunded pension liabilities and overfunded plan assets; and the cash surrender value of life insurance policies. In addition to these items, the accountant must also closely analyze balance sheet adjustments. For example, the adjustment of investment accounts to lower of cost or market; LIFO reserve adjustments; the age and quality of accounts receivables; and the use of aggressive depreciation and amortization methods.

On the side of earnings statements, the accountant must look for areas of hidden or unrecorded earnings and overstated expenses. These can be buried in income (i.e. unrecorded cash receipts), or on the expense side as follows: overstated personal expenses to include travel, entertainment, utilities, etc.; pension expenses and discretionary profit sharing; or related party spin off agreements. Again, the forensic accountant must also closely analyze adjusting entries to the income statement. For example, significant adjustments to officer salaries and deferred bonuses, lease expenses where lease is to related party, and interest on related party debts are all key areas of concern. The adjustment of expenses to industry standards would also signal the accountant of the need for closer review.

This process of delving deeper into the presented financial information requires the accountant to in effect become an investigator. He must learn to question all presented information to ask if it is a valid, correct representation of the financial picture for the company in question. Once these areas are reviewed and opinions formed, the forensic accountant assists the litigating attorney in defending the information in the courtroom in the role of expert witness.

Lost earnings engagements

Another key focus of the forensic accountant in the area of litigation support is lost earning engagements. Lost earnings are defined as "the money the plaintiff would have made but for the actions of the defendant," especially in the areas of personal injury, wrongful death, and damage/loss estimates. To determine lost earnings, the forensic accountant must gather and analyze a variety of information, then provide informed opinions based on the analysis outcomes. This entire process requires the accountant to make a variety of judgment calls, specifically weighing his obligations to the client with those standards established through the CFE and CIRA. Essentially, the accountant is not being paid to support...(a) client's case, but to develop an opinion and then restrict the client's thinking to those issues (the accountant) can support.

To accomplish this goal, the forensic accountant must follow a five-step process to correctly estimate the value of lost earnings. These steps are as follows:

1. Identify an amount to be used as "base earnings"
2. Establish a damage period
3. Identify an appropriate rate of growth;
4. Adjust damages for mitigating circumstances

5. Choose an appropriate discounting technique

Finding an appropriate base earning requires the accountant to identify the amount of revenue being received prior to the incident which caused earnings to cease or decline. Taken into consideration should be revenues from regular operations, special projects, and, in the case of personal injury/wrongful death, the inclusion of appropriate fringe benefits. The accountant must next identify the applicable damage period, or "the time period during which the injured party is expected to experience lost earnings."

Upon establishment of the first two factors, the forensic accountant must next determine an appropriate growth rate. This growth rate would be the "percentage rate that earnings would be expected to increase during the damage period." The accountant would use a variety of sources to determine this rate, including industry standards, historical data, or the Bureau of Labor and Statistics. Once set, the accountant then considers this rate as constant throughout the damage period and moves on to identify mitigating items. Mitigating items offset the monetary value of the damage suffered and can include insurance money received, the effect of income taxes, and the effect of consumption of resources, to name a few.

Finally, the forensic accountant must determine the appropriate discount method. Six methods of discounting are offered for the accountant's use. They include the following methodologies: Traditional discounting; inflation discounting; partial offset discounting; total offset discounting; Supreme Court discounting; and trial and error discounting. Each method requires the quantification of future earnings and the discounting of those earnings to a present value, based on a variety of different factors.

How does a forensic accountant work?

Although each case is distinct and requires accounting and auditing procedures unique to the assignment, many forensic accounting assignments would, include the following steps:

- ▸ *Meet with the client:* The forensic accountant should meet with the client to determine the scope of the engagement. In addition, it is advisable to obtain an engagement letter specifying the terms of the engagement.

- ▸ *Determine independence:* It is understood that a CPA should be independent when performing an audit or other attest services for clients. It is mandatory as well that the forensic accountant be independent, otherwise the credibility of the forensic accountant will be questioned if the engagement results in a legal case.

- ▸ *Plan the engagement:* Proper, advance planning is essential to any type of engagement. The plan should be similar to an audit program, detailing objectives and procedures in a form that addresses the scope of the engagement so that some type of conclusion can be reached.

▶ *Gather evidence and perform analyses:* The forensic accountant should match the auditing, accounting, or investigative technique employed with the type of evidence to be obtained. A specific technique may satisfy more than one objective. When the forensic accountant, for example, performs an audit technique for a particular account, he/she also *finds* evidence for other accounts may be discovered based on the double entry system of accounting. Forensic accountants use a variety of techniques including inquiry, confirmation, physical examination, observation, inspection, reconciliation, tracing, vouching, reperformance, and analytical procedures.

▶ *Make a conclusion and prepare the report:* The forensic accountant should write the final report in a manner that clearly explains the nature of the assignment and the scope of the work. It should indicate the approach used for discovery of information, and detail findings and/or opinions.

Forensic specialists' investigation procedure

In theory, the Enron scandal should never have happened. US financial markets are supposed to be the best regulated in the world, with the Securities and Exchange Commission (SEC) enforcing strict rules on disclosure to protect investors, and private agencies also monitoring companies. But Enron's accounts proved impenetrable to government and private regulators alike, while its main business - energy trading - was only lightly regulated by another set of government agencies which exempted it from many reporting requirements, while maintaining close ties with the company.

Beyond the congressional circus and shredded documents, the fate of the Enron case—and most investigations of suspected corporate crime—rests in the hands of computer forensic experts and forensic accountants working quietly behind the scenes. Investigators will pore through 10,000 computer backup tapes, 20 million sheets of paper and more than 400 computers and handheld devices, according to legal papers. The electronic data is up to 10 times the size of the Library of Congress.

While being equipped with many of the same skills as accountants and computer professionals, forensic detectives in all corporate investigations dig deeper. They mine computer hard drives, financial papers and bank records for "smoking gun" evidence that is allowable in civil and criminal courts. The Justice Department and the Securities and Exchange Commission have launched criminal and civil investigations of Enron and law firms, and their private investigators hope to gather documents for their class-action lawsuits against Enron.

Here is how forensic specialists work big corporate fraud cases, and how the investigation is likely to unfold in the corporate fraud case.

▶ **By tracing the digital and paper trails.** Even if paper documents are trashed, investigators armed with subpoenas can scoop up duplicate papers from the auditor or law firm of the company under investigation. If critical material cannot be found in a company's computer or backup tapes, most large companies keep data in emergency backup systems off-site, in case a natural disaster destroys office records. In addition, investigators with search warrants will seize records, computers, pagers and cell phones from the homes of employees.

▶ **By saving and rebuilding data.** In most corporate fraud cases, investigators will squeeze every bit and byte of data from hard drives, floppy disks, computer tapes and CD-ROMs. Investigators will make copies for storage and to use for their analysis. Often, incriminating documents are deleted, or a suspect will hide records in an unmarked part of a hard drive. Regardless, special software can fish out information.

▶ **By financial profiling.** Some investigators will build financial profiles of suspects and their assets. They study bank documents, tax records and corporate records to chart a suspect's pay, stock options and 401(k) investment holdings. They will interview co-workers, family and friends, and they also will drive by the suspect's home to see if he's living beyond his means.

▶ **By analyzing evidence.** Amid the mountain of records, investigators look for "hot documents" — spreadsheets, invoices, contracts, memos — that show a pattern of suspected wrongdoing. For instance, a company's numbers and quarterly earnings statement might not jibe with accounting standards or past performance. Profit margins might suddenly rise, even though revenue is flat. Or a firm unexpectedly might write off huge amounts of inventory or unsold products.

Investigators in corporate fraud cases also look closely at auditors' work papers, called *past adjusted journal entries (PAJEs)*. PAJEs are journal entries which are not posted to the financial statements and therefore do not tie to the financial statements filed with the SEC. The worksheet with the PAJE's should show a reconciliation from the financials filed with the SEC to what they would have been had the PAJE's been posted.

Forensic computing and the use of technology

In some respects the advances in technology have enabled criminals to commit crimes more quickly and successfully. For example, by capturing database information it is easy to steal people's identity and financial data. The automation of the payroll system has enabled corrupt employees to create false identities to receive pay checks. Deleting a computer file does not necessarily remove the information. Also data stored on one computer may exist in many locations such as on a backup tape, company Blackberry or PDA. Such devices serve as a tape recorder, documenting and storing the evidence of a crime.

The following lists some of basic tools for data detective work.

TOOL	PURPOSE
Network sniffer (hardware)	Allows user to "recreate" the crime by keeping a record of packet sessions across networks.
Portable disk duplicator and/or duplication software	Preserves the original crime scene by allowing investigators to copy hard drives in the field and the lab for later analysis.
Chain-of-custody documentation hardware	Videotapes every mouse click of the investigative process to make court testimony more credible.
Case management software	Helps link seemingly unrelated pieces of evidence.

Phone logs for office, home, fax lines and cell phone may also prove helpful. An employee may try to use a common access phone to make calls. However, employers can also install security access cards to certain areas of the building that have sensitive files. This way an employer can track what employees are accessing.

IT and data mining used to detect corporate fraud

IT tools such as data mining can be effectively employed by fraud auditors. This involves the analysis of data stored in an information system (e.g., a database) to identify patterns that indicate unexplained or potentially questionable transactions. The advantage of such a computer analysis technique is that large numbers of transactions can be evaluated in a relatively short period of time. Further, multiple analyses of individual data elements can be performed to provide different evaluations of potential patterns or trends. Once a pattern is identified, the auditors must further investigate specific transactions to determine whether an improper transaction actually occurred. Data mining can also be very useful in other high-risk corporate processes. Two such areas include executive travel and contract and consulting services.

Cases in forensic accounting

CASE 1—PURCHASE OF A BUSINESS

The following is an actual case in forensic accounting and fraud detection — involving the purchase of a business. The plaintiff alleges that the records shown to him were not accurate and that the lawyer who handled the closing for him was negligent.

MAGYAR, INC.
A Case Study in Fraud

"Since I was a little boy, I wanted to own a business. I never wanted to work for anyone else." Omar Saleem said to his wife, Sylvia.

Omar Saleem was 50 years old, came to the United States 30 years ago, and has worked for a large furniture manufacturer for 28 years. One day, he was reading the classified advertisements of the newspaper and noticed an office business for sale in the next town. He discussed the idea with his wife and she approved. So he contacted the seller and made an appointment. Three days later Omar met with Rahman Magyar, the sole owner of Magyar, Inc. Rahman was an engaging individual, very smooth and personable. Omar was very impressed with Rahman's knowledge of the business and with his self-confidence. Rahman told Omar that he was selling the business because he was bored with it. He had built the company from nothing into a very successful business and now wanted to try something else. Omar believed everything that Rahman said. Rahman said he would be glad to open his books to Omar, but would require a good-faith, refundable deposit of $1,000. Omar agreed and made another appointment for the following week.

Ornar met with Rahman and gave the $1,000 good-faith deposit. Rahman in turn showed Omar his equipment and inventory and explained more about the business. Specifically he told him that he averages about $120,000 per year in office supplies and equipment sales, and about $30,000 in services. The latter is a mail service where he prepares and mails packages for customers. Rahman produced a fee schedule and claimed that this end of the business has been very lucrative. After showing Omar the inventory,

Rahman flashed some papers and tax returns in front of Omar to show him the growth since he opened the business in February 2000. Rahman said that the business has averaged about 20% growth each year. Omar looked at the papers, but actually didn't know what he was looking at. Furthermore, Rahman assured him that the paperwork was in order since his brother-in-law prepared them. He said his brother-in-law, Raj Kupar, was a CPA and that everything was in order. Rahman said that he would sell the business for $160,000, which is less than the normal selling price for this type of business. He said that the selling price is usually one times annual sales. He further said that "since you and I are from the same country, I will help you out. I prefer to sell to you over someone else."

He convinced Omar that he could easily make $75,000 from the business. Furthermore, he suggested that Omar move fast as there were a number of people interested in the business. Omar said that he would have to get an attorney. He promised to get back to Rahman in a week or so. Rahman even suggested an attorney.

Omar was quite excited and couldn't wait to get home to tell his wife. His wife was very supportive. Therefore, Omar asked his good friend, Stanley, if he knew an attorney. Stanley referred him to Neil Klavin, an attorney in town. On the following Monday, Omar called the attorney and made an appointment for Friday of that week. Before the meeting, Omar called Rahman and asked if he would accept $150,000 for the business. Rahman said that he would, but wanted cash and that he would not want to finance the business. Omar said that he had $110,000 in cash, but would require a loan of $40,000. Rahman surprisingly agreed to finance $40,000, but wanted 8% interest. They verbally agreed. Omar said that he was going to see an attorney on Friday to explain the deal. Rahman said "great."

On Friday, Omar went to the attorney, Neil Klavin, with his wife. Omar and the attorney discussed the business deal at length. Klavin said that he would be happy to represent Ornar and would gladly review the contract drawn up by Rahman's attorney. Omar told the attorney that he had seen some documentation regarding income and expenses including the tax returns. Omar told the Klavin that he would like him to review the documentation as well. The attorney said "fine." Omar left the office and then contacted Rahman. He gave Rahman his attorney's name and told him to have his lawyers draw up the paperwork. Omar's wife asked if he was moving a little too fast. Omar said that he had to move fast as it was a good deal and that Rahman had other interested buyers. He felt comfortable that his attorney would say it was a good deal after the attorney reviewed the numbers.

About two weeks later, Neil Klavin received the financial information from Rahman's attorney along with a contract of sale and promissory note for $40,000 at 8% interest. Neil reviewed the information and appeared to find everything in order. Although he did not understand the financials and tax returns that well, he did not suggest to Omar that anything was improper. Nor did he suggest soliciting the help of an expert. For example, he did not suggest contacting a CPA to review the books, financials and tax returns. The closing was scheduled for December 27, 2002. Rahman and Omar appeared at the closing with their wives. The contract and promissory note were signed. Omar was to start on the following Monday. Rahman agreed to stay around for a month to train both Omar and his wife. Since this was a family business (husband and wife), they only had the need for occasional casual labor. Rahman never had a payroll.

Omar showed up on January 2, 2003 eager to learn all about the business. He met Rahman, who turned over the keys to the store. Rahman was very gracious and patient as he explained things to Omar and his wife. This went on for the whole month as agreed upon at closing. During the month, Omar and his wife discussed the relative inactivity. They even mentioned this to Rahman, who replied that January is always slow because it is after the holidays. Rahman said "don't worry as December more than makes up for January." Omar and his wife didn't think too much about it.

Omar was now on his own. He and his wife worked diligently at the business each day. His wife prepared advertisements for the newspaper and ran a number of specials. They methodically kept track of daily revenues and expenses. It became apparent after seven months that the volume was nothing like Rahman had said. They both wondered what they were doing wrong. They were somewhat in denial and did not want to think that they may have been misled and/or tricked. They talked among themselves and decided to talk to an attorney, but not Neil Klavin. Instead they discussed the matter with one of their customers, an attorney named Ted Rich. Ted often went into the store to buy supplies and do special mailings of packages. He took a personal interest in both Omar and his wife, Sylvia. Therefore, he suggested that they make an appointment and discuss the matter further.

Omar and Sylvia talked more about the problem. Another two months went by without any appreciable increase in sales numbers. Finally they made an appointment with Ted Rich. Omar did most of the talking. He also brought copies of all the paperwork that he had including any financial information that he received from Rahman. He also included summaries of his revenues and expenses for the last nine months. They discussed alternatives. Ted asked a number of pertinent questions including whether Omar had an accountant, preferably a CPA, to review the financial information that he received from Rahman. Omar said that he didn't. He said that he gave all the information to his attorney to review. Omar made it clear to Ted that he depended on his attorney, Neil Klavin, for advice. Ted was not in the business of suing other attorneys, however, he was upset that Klavin was so sloppy with the closing. He knew that Omar and his wife were naïve. Nevertheless, that was no excuse for not following due diligence procedures. He believed that Klavin should have realized this and looked out for the welfare of his client. Not wanting to make an immediate decision, Ted told Omar that he would review the information and get back to them in a couple of weeks.

A few days later, Ted reviewed the file and decided that the best way to handle the case was to get an accountant to review the financial information including the tax returns for 2000, 2001, and 2002. Ted called Omar to ask for approval to retain an accountant. Omar agreed.

The next day Ted called George Spyros, a CPA and CFE (certified fraud examiner). George has a small forensic practice and had done work for Ted in the past. Ted and George met for about an hour the following day. George looked at the financial statements and tax returns. The first thing George did was check to see if Rahman's brother-in-law was indeed a CPA. He was not. The reason he did that first was because his cursory review of the tax returns revealed gross preparation errors. It only took George about eight hours to do a detailed review of the paperwork. George then prepared a report for Ted (Exhibit 2).

Ted reviewed the report prepared by Spyros and Company. Based on the report and his discussions with George Spyros, he decided to take the case and pursue suing Neil Klavin. Over the next few months, Ted diligently worked on the case including obtaining interrogatories from a number of individuals including Omar and his wife, Rahman Magyar, and Neil Klavin.

Ted knew that the case was not solid. Therefore, he asked for the opinion of another attorney, Richard Darius of Darius and Spivack. He also asked for a second opinion from Edward Caruso. Both of these attorneys had experience suing other attorneys. Their opinions can be found in Exhibit B and Exhibit C, respectively.

Since the two attorneys had different opinions, Ted thought that it would be in the best interest of his client to try to settle out of court.

EXHIBIT 2

SPYROS AND COMPANY
CERTIFIED PUBLIC ACCOUNTANTS
447 PEARL STREET
WOODBRIDGE, NEW JERSEY 07095

Mr. Theodore R. Rich
400 Pearl Street
Woodbridge, New Jersey 07095

Dear Mr. Rich,

In accordance with your request, we have reviewed the Federal income tax returns (Form 1120) of Magyar, Inc. for the eleven months ended December 31, 2000, and the years ended December 31, 2001 and 2002. The purpose of our review was to obtain reasonable assurance about whether the tax returns are free of material misstatement. Our review included examining the propriety of the amounts presented on the returns based on analytical procedures. Specifically, we have determined that:

(1) The company employed the accrual basis of accounting (see box checked on page 2 of the 2000 return). Since the balance sheets each year do not show any accounts receivable or accounts payable, one can logically conclude that all revenues and expenses were for cash.

(2) Based on the conclusion reached in (1) above, the cash balances reflected on the balance sheets on page 4 of the 2001 and 2002 tax returns are not reasonable. This fact can be supported by the following reconciliation:

Increase (decrease) in cash—

    Cash balance at inception$—

Issuance of stock in 2000	7,536
Loans in 2000	29,438
Equipment	(16,251)
Sales	101,792
Cost of sales	(118,326)
Expenses (excluding depreciation of $638)	(25,812)
Cash balance on December 31, 2000 should be	$(21,623)
Cash balance on December 31, 2000 per tax return	$ 250

Comments:
It is unreasonable for cost of sales to be more than sales.
Cash is misstated by $21,873

Recalculated cash balance on January 1, 2001	$ (21,623)
Additional issuance of stock in 2001	23,960
Payoff of loans	(29,438)
Sales	141,158
Cost of sales	(139,617)
Expenses (excluding depreciation of $638	(38,102)
Cash balance on December 31, 2001 should be	$ (63,662)
Cash balance on December 31, 2001 per tax return	$ 250

Comments:
It is unreasonable for cost of sales to be 99% of sales.
Cash is misstated cumulatively by $63,912

Recalculated cash balance on January 1, 2002	$ (63,662)
Sales	157,572
Cost of sales	(145,710)
Expenses (excluding depreciation of $638	(24,417)
Cash balance on December 31, 2002 should be	$(76,217)
Cash balance on December 31, 2002 per tax return	$295

Comments:
It is unreasonable for cost of sales to be 93% of sales.
Cash is misstated cumulatively by $76,512

We also compared the tax returns to the internal financial statements prepared by Raj Kupar, who we understand is a CPA and brother-in-law of the prior owner of the business, Rahman Magyar. Please be advised that we could not find a relationship between the financial statements and the tax returns. The tax returns were materially different from the internal financial statements. Revenues on the internal financials were approximately $15,000 higher in 2000, $18,000 lower in 2001 and $30,000 higher in 2002. There appeared to be only a partial listing of expenses, such that 2000 showed a profit of $70,000, 2001 a profit of $65,000 and 2002 a profit of $74,000. The costs and expenses were substantially less than those shown on the tax returns. In addition, the tax returns reflected substantial losses each year. Finally, the internal financial statements were not prepared in accordance with generally accepted accounting principles.

You also asked us to check whether or not Mr. Kupar is a practicing CPA in New Jersey. We did check with the New Jersey State Board of Public Accountants. He is neither a licensed CPA nor licensed public accountant.

Thank you for the opportunity of serving you. If you have any questions about this report, please contact us directly.

Woodbridge, New Jersey
July 24, 2004

EXHIBIT 3

DARIUS AND SPIVACK
One Main Street
Hackensack, NJ 07601

March 25, 2005

Theodore R. Rich, Esq.
100 Pearl Street
Woodbridge, New Jersey 07095

Re:Saleem v. Klavin

Dear Mr. Rich:

This report relates to an action for legal malpractice brought by your clients, **Omar and Sylvia Saleem against Neil Klavin,** a member of the New Jersey Bar. It derives from your request for my opinion as to whether third party defendant Klavin breached any duty to his former clients, the third party plaintiffs herein, when he undertook to represent them in July, 2002, with respect to the purchase of a certain office supply and mail box business, known as Magyar, Inc., located at 189 Princeton Road, Woodbridge, New Jersey.

For purposes of this report, I have read, analyzed and relied upon multiple documents contained in all your litigation files, including the February, 9, 2004 depositions of Omar Saleem, Sylvia Saleem and Rahman Magyar; the December 27, 2002 Contract of Sale between Magyar, Inc., and Omar and Sylvia Saleem; the January 4, 2003 addendum to closing statement; the January 2, 2003 Lease between Magyar, Inc. and Marjama Company; Rahman Magyar's answers to interrogatories; the December 27, 2002 note from Omar and Sylvia Saleem to Rahman Magyar; correspondence between attorneys D'Orio (for seller) and Klavin (for buyer) dated respectively October 14, 2002 and November 2, 2002 and December 3, 2002. Kindly note that the documents listed above do not include all the materials examined by me, such as all correspondence between and among the parties, all pleadings, all discovery, and the like. Most especially did I review and analyze the July 24, 2004 expert report of Spyros and Company, Certified Public Accountants, rendered on behalf of Omar and Sylvia Saleem.

STATEMENT OF FACTS

In early 2002, Omar Saleem, a native of Syria, but living and working in the United States since 1966, expressed interest in buying a small business. He read about a business for sale in the local newspaper. He answered the advertisement and soon met one Rahman Magyar, the owner of Magyar, Inc., a company engaged in the office supply and mail service business. Later, at a meeting held in Radman Magyar's office, Omar verbally said that he was interested in purchasing the business. About a week later Saleem called Magyar. The two agreed on a price of $150,000 including a $40,000 promissory note to Magyar. During the course of the preliminary negotiations, Magyar had assured the Saleems that the business was a very simple operation which they would have no problem understanding and that he would agree to work a month in the business free of charge to train both Omar and his wife. For whatever reason, Magyar never offered the Saleems an opportunity to examine the books and records of the Company, or to have them examined by an outside accountant. However, he did show them some tax returns and financial statements prepared by his brother-in-law, whom he alleged was a CPA. After the closing, Magyar did provide on the job training, but it was hurried and did not afford the Saleems hardly any opportunity to understand the economics of the business.

The essential complaint of the Saleems is that their attorney Klavin failed to provide them with appropriate legal advice and counsel in connection with the actual purchase of the business. In this regard the Saleems contend that Klavin failed to incorporate certain conditions and contingencies in the December 27, 2003 contract which would have made the sale subject to a review of all books, records, income tax returns, and the like, by a Certified Public Accountant acting on behalf of the buyers. Thus, instead of advising the Saleems not to sign the contract and make any substantial deposit until the Saleems had all the books and records examined by their accountant; and having, alternatively, failed to incorporate such protective contingencies and conditions in the contract, Klavin put his clients on the horns of a dilemma faced, as they unfortunately were, with either losing their $1,000 deposit or purchasing the business in total ignorance of its monthly income and expenses.

CONCLUSIONS OF LAW

The matter of attorney negligence arising out of this matter, must, of course, be evaluated and judged in accordance with the standard of care applicable in legal malpractice actions. In this regard, it is settled that an attorney is obligated to exercise on behalf of his client the knowledge, skill and ability ordinarily possessed and exercised by members of the legal profession similarly situated, and to employ reasonable care and prudence in connection therewith. *McCullough v. Sullivan,* 102 N.J.L. 381, 384 (E. & A. 1926); *Sullivan v. Stoudt,* 120 N.J.L. 304, 308 (E. &A. 1938; *Taylor v. Shepard,* 136 NJ Super. 85,90 (App. Div. 1982) ; *Saint Pius X House of Retreats v. Camden Diocese,* 88 N.J. 571, 588, (1982). Perhaps the most quoted statement of the rule of care applicable to attorney negligence suits is found in *Hodges v. Carter,* 239 N.C. 517, 80 S.E. 2nd 144 (1954):

"Ordinarily when an attorney engages in the practice of the law and contracts to prosecute an action in behalf of his client, he impliedly represents that (1) he possesses the requisite degree of learning, skill and ability necessary to the practice of his profession and which others similarly situated ordinarily possess; (2) he will exercise his best judgment in the prosecution of the litigation entrusted to him and (3) he will exercise into reasonable and ordinary care and diligence in the use of his skill and in the application of his knowledge to his client's cause? (Id. at 519, 80 S.E. 2nd at 145146).

What constitutes a reasonable degree of care is not to be considered in a vacuum. On the contrary, it must be the facts and circumstances of each specific case, and the type of service the attorney undertakes therein. With this in mind, I now proceed to examine the conduct of the subject defendant attorney in connection with his professional duties and conduct in the management of the above matter.

The record shows an egregious failure on the part of attorney Klavin to safeguard and protect the interests of his clients when he undertook to represent them in the purchase of Magyar, Inc. This conclusion is based upon the fact that defendant Klavin made no attempt to follow the standard and elementary procedures mandated for any attorney representing a buyer in the acquisition of a corporation. Thus, if Klavin had truly represented the interests of the Saleems, he would not only have examined all Magyar Inc's Federal and State tax returns, he would also, as a part of that investigation, have conducted a lien search in every place that Magyar conducted its business; would have obtained from Magyar an up to date financial statement in order to understand the economic aspects of the deal; would have obtained an independent audit of that financial statement; would have checked the terms, acceleration clauses and restrictions on any notes or mortgages or other indebtedness of the corporation; would have examined all insurance policies to discover what unknown liabilities existed; would have examined the viability and collectability of all accounts receivable; would have made a complete physical inventory of all corporate assets, together with a current market evaluation of same; would have examined the important contracts of Magyar and its customers, which constituted the life blood of that corporation; and would have performed other common sense duties, such as talking to the main customers of Magyar, all for the over all purpose of insuring that the interests of his clients, the Saleems, were fully protected and safeguarded.

It is my opinion that if Klavin had conducted this type of basic and common sense investigation, as he was bound to do in accordance with his duties as an attorney of this state, the Saleems would not have undertaken to purchase Magyar, and would thereby have escaped all the financial damage, loss of time, mental stress and anguish which they unfortunately suffered as a result of this purchase. Indeed, we now know that as a direct result of his negligence, Klavin caused his clients to lose at least $110,000 due to the misrepresentations made by the seller. In short, I find on the facts and the law that defendant Klavin, in his attorney client relationship with the Saleems, fell below the standard of care and prudence exercised by ordinary members of the New Jersey Bar. Otherwise put, attorney Klavin, in his relationship with the Saleems, deviated substantially from the standard of care expected of New Jersey attorneys.

But it remains basic to the Saleems' cause of action for legal malpractice that the wrongful conduct or failures of attorney Klavin are a proximate cause of their injuries. In order to establish "causation", the burden is clearly upon the Saleems to prove that the negligence of Klavin was "more likely than not" a substantial factor in causing the unfavorable result. *Lecral Malpractice, Mallen & Levit,* at pg. 502; and also see *Lieberman v. Employers Ins. of Wassau,* 85 N.J. 325, 341 (1980) ; *Hoppe* y. Ranzini, 58 N.J. Super. 233, 238239 (App. Div. 1975), certif. den. 70 N.J. 144 (1976); *Lamb y. Barbour,* 188 N.J. Super. 6, 12 (App. Div. 1982) ; and as to the test of proximate cause see *State y Jersey Central Power & Light Co.* ,69 N.J. 102, 100(1976); *Ettin y. Ava Truck Leasing Inc.,* 153 N.J. 463,483(1969) . And plaintiff is obliged to carry this burden of proof by the presentation of competent, credible evidence, which proves material facts; and not conjecture, surmise or suspicion. *Lang y. Landy,* 35 N.J. 44, 54 (1961) ; *Modla v. United States, 15* F. Supp. 198, 201, (D.N.J. 1957). Otherwise stated, third party plaintiffs herein must establish a chain of causation between their damages and the negligence or other wrongful conduct on the part of defendant Klavin. *Catto v. Schnepp,* 21 N.J. supra. 506, 511 (App. Div.) affld o.b. 62 N.J. 20 (1972).

Based upon the facts presented to me, and the applicable law, it is my view that the inexplicable failure of defendant Klavin to inspect or provide for the inspection of all Magyar, Inc. tax returns and corporate books and records, were the immediate factors that caused the Saleems to sustain heavy losses. It follows, therefore, that third party defendant Klavin is liable to the third party plaintiffs Saleems for legal malpractice and all causally related damages.

Very truly yours,

Richard M. Darius

EXHIBIT 4

EDWARD J. CARUSO
Counselor at Law
300 Broad Street
Newark, New Jersey 07104

June 8, 2005

Theodore R. Rich, Esq.
100 Pearl Street
Woodbridge, New Jersey 07095

Re:Saleem v. Klavin

Dear Mr. Rich:

Please be advised that this opinion relates to an action for legal malpractice brought by your clients, Omar and Sylvia Saleem against Neil Klavin, a member of the New Jersey Bar. It derives from your request for my opinion as to whether third party defendant Klavin breached any duty to his former clients, the third party plaintiffs herein, when he undertook to represent them in July, 2002, with respect to the purchase of a certain office supply and mail box business, known as Magyar, Inc., located at 189 Princeton Road, Woodbridge, New Jersey. For purposes of this report, I have read, analyzed and relied upon the following documents contained in all your litigation files:

- ▶ February, 9, 2004 depositions of Omar Saleem, Sylvia Saleem and Rahman Magyar;
- ▶ December 27, 2002 Contract of Sale between Magyar, Inc., and Omar and Sylvia Saleem;
- ▶ January 4, 2003 addendum to closing statement;
- ▶ January 2, 2003 Lease between Magyar, Inc. and Marjama Company; Rahman Magyar answers to interrogatories;
- ▶ December 27, 2002 note from Omar and Sylvia to Rahman Magyar; correspondence between attorneys D'Orio (for seller) and Klavin (for buyer) dated respectively October 14, 2002 and November 2, 2002 and December 3, 2002.

▶ July 24, 2004 expert report prepared by the CPA firm of Spyros and Company; and

▶ March 25, 2005 expert opinion of Darius and Spivack

Also please note that the documents listed above do not include all the materials examined by me, such as all correspondence between and among the parties, all pleadings, all discovery, and the like.

I have reviewed the documents referred to above in order to provide you with my opinion as to whether Neil Klavin deviated from the standard of care, which would be applicable in this transaction. Based on my review of all the documents set forth above, I am of the opinion that Mr. Klavin did not deviate from the standard of care for the reasons set forth below.

The transaction that is the subject of the litigation and this report involved the purchase of a business known as Magyar, Inc. The plaintiffs, Omar and Sylvia Saleem, executed a contract to purchase the aforesaid business from Magyar, Inc. In connection with the original negotiations relative to the business, the plaintiffs received a document showing projection of income and return on equity in connection with the business. This document was reviewed by the plaintiffs prior to the execution of the contract. The document was, in fact, executed by both of the plaintiffs, namely Omar and Sylvia Saleern.

After the parties agreed on all relevant terms for the transaction, the seller's attorney, Louis D'Orb, prepared a contract of sale. Ultimately, the contract was taken to Mr. Klavin by Omar Saleem. After reviewing the contract, Klavin prepared a review letter dated November 2, 2002. The review letter set forth a number of contingencies including, but not limited to, the following:

1. Review and approval of the existing lease.
2. A requirement that the buyer be permitted to review the books of the seller.
3. Inclusion in the contract of a more detailed listing of scheduled assets

The response to Mr. Klavin's letter was Mr. D'Orio's letter dated December 3, 2002. In that letter Mr. D'Orio advised Mr. Klavin that a lease contingency was not necessary since the lease had already been reviewed and approved by Mr. Klavin's clients. Mr. Klavin did question his clients in connection with the aforesaid lease and ultimately was satisfied that his clients read, understood, and were willing to accept same.

The next item discussed in Mr. D'Orio's letter was Mr. Klavin's request that his clients be permitted access to the books and records of the selling corporation. Mr. D'Orio requested that the review period be limited to five days and that there be some ascertainable standard as to whether or not the review was "acceptable" or "unacceptable." In the last section of his letter, Mr. D'Orio provides Mr. Klavin with a more detailed schedule of assets.

It is obvious that the contents of Mr. D'Orio's letter were reviewed by Mr. Klavin and further reviewed by Mr. Klavin with his clients. I note that Mr. D'Orio requested that Mr. Klavin and/or his clients execute the letter so same could be incorporated as a part of the contract. I further note that Mr. Klavin, in fact, had his clients execute the letter after he reviewed same with him.

It is interesting that when Mr. Klavin forwarded the December 3, 2002 letter, which was executed by his clients, he included a cover letter in an effort to resolve the issue relative to a satisfactory review of the books and records. In that letter, Mr. Klavin indicates that his clients' review of the books would be acceptable provided the books and records indicate gross receipts in excess of $175,000. I believe it is unequivocally clear that Mr. Klavin was sensitive to his clients' needs to review the books and records and furthermore had a discussion with his clients in connection with same. Stated another way, Mr. Klavin had placed his clients in a position where they were able to have access to the books and records before performing the contract.

In addition, the other elements of the transaction, including lease review, etc., were all properly handled by Mr. Klavin. All of the critical issues in connection with the purchase of a business were considered and reviewed with the client and were also the subject of informed consent.

In the opinion letter of Darius and Spivak, Mr. Darius suggests that "Klavin failed to incorporate certain conditions and contingencies in the December 27, 2002 contract, which would have made the sale subject to a review of all books. . . " This obviously is inapposite to the existing fact pattern, since the letter of December 3, 2002 clearly incorporates that contingency. Mr. Darius goes on to indicate that Mr. Klavin should have advised the Saleems not to sign the contract and make a deposit until the Saleems had all the books and records examined by their accountant. This simply flies in the face of the normal business practice in connection with the sale of a business. Having conducted numerous business closings over my 31 years of practice, it is my opinion that it would be extremely unusual to be involved in a transaction where a seller would let a buyer review books on any basis unless a substantial good faith deposit was made and a contract was executed by the parties.

Finally, Mr. Darius suggests that Mr. Klavin put his clients, "on the horns of a dilemma," which resulted in their being faced with either losing a deposit or purchasing a business in total ignorance of the monthly income. This dilemma was not created by Klavin. Mr. Klavin clearly gave his clients the opportunity to have the books and records reviewed. He received representations from his clients that they were reviewed and understood. If Mr. Klavin's clients had, in fact, performed their due diligence and reviewed the books and were unsatisfied with the result of their review, the contract could have been voided provided the review occurred within the contractual period. It was only at the day of the closing that the plaintiffs first indicated that *they* had not had an opportunity to review the books and records of the corporation.

At that point, Mr. Klavin properly advised his clients that in the event they refused to consummate the transaction, they faced a possible loss of their deposit, and possibly other damages for breach of contract, since they did not avail themselves of the accounting contingency within the time period set forth in the contract.

I note that Mr. Darius states in his report "that if Klavin had truly represented the interest of the Saleems, he would not only have examined all Magyar's Federal and State tax returns; he would also, as part of the investigation, have conducted a lien search..." It appears that Mr. Darius is suggesting that Mr. Klavin should fulfill the role of an accountant and examine the books and records of the corporation. This is simply not an accurate statement, nor an accurate reflection of the duty of a closing attorney. Insofar as the lien search is concerned, same was, in fact, conducted by Mr. Klavin, who ordered what is the normal and customary business search in connection with the proposed closing.

Mr. Darius goes on to indicate in his letter various undertakings that should have been performed by Mr. Klavin. Many of the undertakings set forth in Mr. Darius' letter do not fall in the ambit of a lawyer's duty to his client. Many of the functions would be performed by an accountant or other professional and not within the scope of a duty owed by an attorney to his client.

In the case at bar, I believe it is clear from the deposition transcript and the correspondence referred to above, that Mr. Klavin adequately performed these duties.

Very truly yours,

Edward J. Caruso

Case 2 — Tracing the Money Trail of Terrorism

Forensic accounting has been essential post 9/11. Many of the businesses housed in the World Trade Center lost their records. Payrolls, expenditures, and receipts for assets needed to be accounted for in order to file insurance claims. Forensic accountants have also been tracing how money made its way to the terrorists as well as those who had advance notice of the terrorism and profited from the tragedy. Interestingly, much of the money funding Middle East terrorism is not laundered but comes from clean sources such as charitable organizations.

'Forensic accountants' dig through financial records for proof of hijackers' link to Bin Laden's network. Accountants, computer experts and fraud investigators have risen to the forefront of the new war against terrorism.

Though physical targets are difficult to identify, federal officials realized that the flow of money to terrorists is a key vulnerability in their underground networks.

One of the first acts by the federal government after the attacks on the World Trade Center and the Pentagon was the creation of the Foreign Terrorist Asset Tracking Center--a group of financial investigators drawn from the CIA, FBI, National Security Agency, U.S. Customs Service, Secret Service and other government agencies. They already have spent 11 days poring over bank records, credit card statements, transactions from brokerage accounts and other financial information in search of links between the 19 men who hijacked four jetliners on Sept. 11 and various organizations connected to Osama bin Laden's Al Qaeda network.

The U.S. government is optimistic that this type of strategic approach to funding of terrorist activity will serve as a preventive approach to dismantling terrorist activities before they even begin. They face a daunting puzzle that grows exponentially with each step backward through the financial records. The field is known as "forensic accounting." Its usual role is in securities fraud investigations, embezzlement cases and divorce proceedings in which one spouse suspects the other of hiding assets. Traditionally, the role of accountants is to collect financial data and organize the information into a single comprehensive financial statement.

A forensic accountant typically begins with a single credit card receipt, such as one showing the signature of Mohamed Atta, believed to have been one of the hijackers of American Airlines Flight 11. The receipt, from Warrick's Rent-a-Car in Pompano Beach, Fla., contains a credit card number linked to a specific account. The transactions on that account can reveal a pattern that may lead to other conspirators.

The records also will indicate how purchases were paid for, most likely with a check. That will lead to a bank account, belonging to either the suspect or one of his financial patrons.

The key is tracking the flow of money in and out of the account. If funds came in by check, the account number on that check can be traced. If money was wired into the account, the source of those funds could be identified as well. Canceled checks will reveal the account numbers of people who received money from the suspect.

Each account could be linked to several others, which in turn could have links to yet more accounts. An investigation could quickly reveal a network with multiplying branches and perhaps hundreds or even thousands of leads.

Other kinds of financial transactions also could become the starting point for new branches.

For example, tracking center investigators are trying to figure out who purchased put options in American Airlines and United Airlines in the days before the attacks involving the companies' planes. The put options would rise in value if the prices of those airline stocks fell in subsequent weeks.

Indeed, shares of American parent AMR Corp. have sunk 40% since the attacks, and shares of United parent UAL Corp. have plummeted 44%.

Investigators are suspicious that some of the buyers knew about the attacks in advance. Finding them could lead to sources of terrorist funding, said Lewis Freeman, a forensic accountant based in Miami.

The biggest potential roadblock in tracing the trail of money is the use of cash. The Bank Secrecy Act requires banks and other businesses to file a currency transaction report with the federal government whenever they conduct a transaction or series of transactions involving at least $10,000 in cash. But the act is easily circumvented by spreading out deposits so they are below that threshold.

There is simply too much cash in circulation for investigators to be able to determine where any specific bills came from.

The use of false identification also could cause a trail to end abruptly. U.S. banks typically require a government-issued picture ID, such as a driver's license or a passport, to open an account. But banks aren't usually on the lookout for false IDs, and someone with a reasonable fake probably wouldn't encounter any problems, said Ray, the former FBI special agent.

Investigators may have no trouble tracing the source of funds to a specific bank account—-but then find that those banks are based in Syria, Iraq, Libya or even Afghanistan. Those countries aren't likely to cooperate with U.S. investigators.

Still, investigators have many advantages. They should be able to conduct their investigation much more rapidly than normal forensic accountants, which will allow them to make progress before leads grow stale.

Public records will be made available to them more quickly than to their counterparts in the private sector. And as agents of the government, they have access to more sources of information.

Perhaps the most potent weapon the investigators have is time. The government can afford to track down as many leads as they can uncover. Forensic accountants said there was no way to predict how long it would take for the tracking center to identify and cut off funds for terrorism. Most agreed it would be impossible to trace every single money trail to its source. But eventually, they are almost certain to disrupt the money flow and potentially forestall at least some future terrorist attacks.

Certifications

What does it take to become a forensic accountant? There is a need for the same basic accounting skills that it takes to become a good auditor plus the ability to pay attention to the smallest detail, analyze data thoroughly, think creatively, possess common business sense, be proficient with a computer, and have excellent communication skills. A "sixth sense" that can be used to reconstruct details of past accounting transactions is also beneficial. A photographic memory helps when trying to visualize and reconstruct these past events. The forensic accountant also needs the ability to maintain his composure when detailing these events on the witness stand. Finally, a forensic accountant should be insensitive to personal attacks on his professional credibility. In addition to these personal characteristics, accountants must meet several additional requirements to gain the position of forensic accountant.

To become a qualified forensic accountant there are several degrees, certifications, and positions that serve as to qualify the accountant as an 'expert' in this field. Forensic accountants, who are usually involved in litigation support or investigative accounting, must have some form of credentials to deem them capable of the work or career they are pursuing. After completion of the basic requirements for an undergraduate degree, there are two main professional certifications that are now available. They are the Certified Fraud Examiner (CFE) and the Certified Insolvency and Reorganization Accountant (CIRA).

Certified Fraud Examiners

The Association of Certified Fraud Examiners (**www.acfe.org**), established in 1988, is based in Austin, Texas. The 50,000-member professional organization is dedicated to educating qualified individuals (Certified Fraud Examiners), who are trained in the highly specialized aspects of detecting, investigating, and deterring fraud and white-collar crime. Each member of the Association designated a Certified Fraud Examiner (CFE) has earned certification after an extensive application process and upon passing the uniform CFE Examination.

Certified Fraud Examiners come from various professions, including auditors, accountants, fraud investigators, loss prevention specialists, attorneys, educators, and criminologists. CFEs gather evidence, take statements, write reports, and assist in investigating fraud in its varied forms. CFEs are employed by most major corporations and government agencies, and others provide consulting and investigative services.

The Association sponsors approximately 100 local chapters worldwide. CFEs in over 70 countries on four continents have investigated more than 1,000,000 suspected cases of civil and criminal fraud. In order to gain the CFE designation, you must pass the CFE Exam. The 500 question exam is designed to measure your academic as well as practical knowledge in four main areas: Criminology and Ethics, Financial Transactions, Legal Elements of Fraud and Fraud Examination and Investigation. Like other tests, the difficulty can vary widely, based upon individual circumstances such as experience and preparation.

Sample Questions

Criminology and Ethics

1. Given all of the following fraud prevention methods within organizations, which one is probably the most effective?
    A. Reducing rationalization
    B. Having an open-door policy
    C. Increasing the perception of detection
    D. Screening employees

2. One of the first steps in determining if financial statements contain fraudulent entries is to find out if the equality of the debits and credits has been maintained. In order to accomplish this task, which one of the following should be examined?
    A. The trial balance
    B. The income statement
    C. The balance sheet
    D. The statement of cash flows

3. Cain, the authorized signer on his company's accounts, prepared and signed a check payable to the company's plumber. He gave the check to Baker, his secretary, and asker her to mail the check to the plumber. Instead, Baker took the check home, signed the plumber's name on the back and had her husband cash the check at their grocery store. According to Occupational Fraud and Abuse, Baker committed which of the following schemes?
    A. An altered payee scheme
    B. A forged endorsement scheme
    C. A forged maker scheme
    D. An authorized maker scheme

Answer 1 (C)

Increasing the perception of detection may well be the most effective fraud prevention method. Controls, for example, do little good in forestalling internal theft and fraud if their presence is not known by those at risk. In the audit profession, this means letting employees, managers, and executives know that auditors are actively seeking out information concerning internal theft.

Answer 2 (A)

The equality of debits and credits in the ledger should be verified at the end of each accounting period, if not more often. If fraudulent financial statements are suspected, a verification of the equality of debits and credits also is one of the first steps. Frauds often result in books that don't balance. Such a verification, which is called a trial balance, may be in the form of a calculator tape or in the form of a summary listing of both the balances and the titles of the accounts used in preparing the financial statements. The trial balance does not provide complete proof of the accuracy of the ledger. It indicates only that the debits and the credits are equal. This proof is of value, however, because errors frequently affect the equality of debits and credits.

Answer 3 (B)

Forged endorsement frauds are those check tampering schemes in which an employee intercepts a company check intended for a third party and converts the check by signing the third party's name on the endorsement line of the check.

Certified Insolvency and Reorganization Accountant (CIRA)

The second certification which is available to the forensic accountant is the CIRA. It is administered by the Association of Insolvency and Restructuring Advisors (AIRA) (www.aira.org).To complete the requirements for the CIRA, the accountant must have attained at least five years of professional accounting experience. These five years must be spent in a public accounting firm and 4,000 hours must be accumulated in insolvency and reorganizational accounting. The actual exam for the CIRA is different from any other certification in the accounting profession. There are three parts to the exam. The areas of concentration are: financial reporting and taxes; managing turnaround and bankruptcy cases; and plan development and accounting.

Implications

A key to the study and training for forensic accountants and the CFE and CIRA certifications in the future should be directly related to the systems demands of our society. We currently have over one million pages being created and added to the Internet every month, with a total annual estimate of 12-15 million pages this year. With this influx of data, the occurrence of computer related crime and fraud will continue to increase dramatically, and therefore the need to prepare professionals to combat this new crime is pressing. As a result of this new demand, universities need to enhance (and in some cases, commence) a course of study to prepare future accountants for the CFE and CIRA, just as they currently do for the CPA exam.

Indicators of Financial Crime

Red Flags of Employee Behavior

1. **Overworking** – financial criminals are sophisticated, and know that the typical suspects of misdeeds in organizations are likely to be those who miss work a lot, call in sick, go home early, and so forth. Hence, the financial criminal (also by inclination) tends to work long and hard, staying after hours, volunteering for extra duties, or in short, attempting to appear as a superstar in the organization. This is called the protective behavior pattern.

2. **Overpersonalized business matters** – a financial criminal will become extremely upset over little things that touch on or threaten their scam or fraud, and this may be something as minor as a change in office location, or something like another employee dealing with a vendor that only they think they should be dealing with. They may also not have kind words to say about top management (calling them corrupt) because (a) they want to be perceived as a powerbroker or dealmaker, and (b) they plan to claim, if caught, that the kind of thing they did was nothing compared to what goes on at the top.

3. **Antisocial loner personality** – the criminal may or may not have this personality to begin with, but criminologists say that something about the unshareable aspects of financial crime may cause the person to become a loner. Their constant griping (see #2) about top management and how

screwed up the workplace is also tends to result in a perception that they are antisocial. Their relationships with co-workers can be characterized as cold and impersonal since all they are inquisitive about is how co-workers do their job so they can learn about any system controls that are in place throughout the organization.

4. **Inappropriate lifestyle change** – few financial criminals can resist the urge to spend some of their ill-gained loot, and their lifestyle, assets, travel, or offshore bank accounts will just not add up to the salary they're making. They are driven by money and ego, and if given the chance, will jump at almost every opportunity to make more money, and to boast and brag about knowing such opportunities.

Red Flags of Organizational Behavior

1. **Unrealistic performance compensation packages** – the organization will rely almost exclusively, and to the detriment of employee retention, on executive pay systems linked to the organization's profit margins or share price.

2. **Inadequate Board oversight** – there is no real involvement by the Board of Directors, Board appointments are honorariums for the most part, and conflicts of interest as well as nepotism (the second cousin to corruption) are overlooked.

3. **Unprofitable offshore operations** – foreign operation facilities that should be closed down are kept barely functioning because this may be where top management fraudsters have used bribes to secure a "safe haven" in the event of need for swift exit.

4. **Poor segregation of duties** – the organization does not have sufficient controls on who has budget authority, who can place requisitions, or who can take customer orders, and who settles or reconciles these things when the expenses, invoices, or receipts come in.

5. **Poor computer security** – the organization doesn't seem to care about computer security, has slack password controls, hasn't invested in antivirus, firewalls, IDS, logfiles, data warehousing, data mining, or the budget and personnel assigned to IS. Simultaneously, the organization seems over-concerned with minor matters, like whether employees are downloading music, chatting, playing games, or viewing porn.

6. **Low morale, high staff turnover, and whistleblowers** – Low morale and staff shortages go hand-in-hand, employees feel overworked and underpaid,

frequent turnover seems to occur in key positions, and complaints take the form of whistleblowing.

Source: Adapted from "Investigative Methods in Forensic Accounting" an online article by Tom O'Connor. (http://www.apsu.edu/oconnort/3220/3220lect08b.htm)

Red Flags of Money Laundering or Terrorist Financing

Red flags that may indicate money laundering or terrorist financing by individuals, businesses, or financial institutions

- ▶ A foreign entity is willing to sell material at deep discounts or purchase resalable material at top dollar.
- ▶ A party repeatedly purchases highly valuable assets (e.g., precious stones and gems, precious metals, and collectibles) without a clear business purpose (e.g., buying valuable antiques at auctions).
- ▶ An entity conducts an activity incongruent with its business (e.g., a clothing retailer that records revenue for a large wire transfer).
- ▶ A customer or supplier exhibits unusual concern or secrecy, especially with regard to business assets or dealings with other firms.
- ▶ A customer or supplier has difficulty describing the business and lacks general knowledge of his or her industry.
- ▶ A customer or supplier appears to act for an undisclosed principal and refuses to identify that entity or person.
- ▶ A customer finances a big-ticket item and makes accelerated payments on the loan, evading the filing of proper documentation.
- ▶ A customer or supplier uses an informal money transfer network or money transmitter with no apparent business justification.
- ▶ A customer or supplier travels to a country where he or she has no business or family ties or that is not a vacation destination.
- ▶ A customer purchases expensive items (e.g., vehicles, real estate, boats, aircraft, collectibles, and precious gems and metals) in the names of family members or third parties without any apparent logical justification.
- ▶ A customer has financial transactions involving nonprofit or charitable entities that have no logical economic purpose, or there is no link between the entity's stated activity and the other parties in the transaction.
- ▶ A customer transfers funds to or from foreign "shell" entities.

▶ A customer retains a safe deposit box on behalf of a commercial or charitable entity although the entity's activities do not appear to justify the use of a safe deposit box.

▶ A customer opens several bank accounts in the names of family members and deposits small amounts of currency in these accounts regularly. The deposited amounts might be less than $1,000 on a daily basis or $2,000 to $3,000 several times weekly

▶ A customer has account activity showing numerous currency, cashier's check, money order, or traveler's check transactions totaling significant sums.

▶ A customer provides false information.

▶ A customer repeatedly uses a bank account as a temporary resting place for funds from multiple sources without a clear business purpose.

▶ A customer purchases monetary instruments such as money orders, traveler's checks, bank drafts, cashier's checks, or bank checks in amounts below $3,000 or $10,000, possibly to avoid filing the required paperwork.

▶ A customer bulk ships currency to a jurisdiction with secrecy laws.

▶ A customer opens a bank account for which several persons have signature authority, yet these persons appear to have no ties to each other.

▶ A customer opens an account in the name of a new business or entity and in which a higher than expected level of deposits is made in comparison to the entity's revenues.

▶ A customer opens an account for a legal entity that has the same address as other legal entities for which the same person (or persons) has signature authority without legal or business justification (e.g., individuals serving as directors for multiple companies at the same location).

▶ A customer makes use of an informal money transfer network or money transmitter with no apparent business justification.

▶ A customer opens multiple accounts into which numerous small deposits are made that are not collectively commensurate with the customer's income.

▶ A customer engages in transactions involving foreign currency exchanges that are followed within a short time by wire transfers to locations of concern.

▶ A customer uses multiple accounts to collect and channel funds to a small number of foreign beneficiaries in locations of concern.

▶ A customer secures a credit instrument or engages in financial transactions involving moving funds to or from given locations for which there is no logical business or personal reason.

- A customer opens an account in a location of concern without a business purpose.
- A customer has a dormant account holding a minimal sum that suddenly receives a deposit or series of deposits followed by daily cash withdrawals that continue until the deposited sum is removed.
- A customer makes unusual or frequent use of trusts. (Such devices have limited potential for abuse at the placement stage of the money laundering process but greater potential at the layering and integration stages.)
- A customer purchases a single-premium life insurance policy and then immediately borrows against the cash surrender value.
- A customer makes large cash withdrawals from a business account not normally associated with cash transactions.
- A customer makes deposits for a business in combinations of monetary instruments that are atypical of the activity normally associated with such a business.
- A customer carries out multiple transactions on the same day at the same branch of a financial institution, attempting to use different tellers.
- A customer, using accomplices, makes deposits through multiple branches of the same financial institution at the same time.
- A customer makes deposits or withdrawals of cash in amounts that consistently fall just below a reporting threshold.
- A customer makes wire transfers in small amounts in an apparent attempt to avoid triggering identification or report filing.
- A customer authorizes a third party to make foreign exchange transactions followed by wire transfers of the funds to nations of concern or to locations having no apparent business connection with the customer.
- A customer has accounts in, or has wire transfers to or from, a bank secrecy haven or nation identified as a money laundering risk.
- A customer has funds wired to or through a U.S. financial institution from a foreign source, and then the money is withdrawn using ATMs in a third country.
- A customer receives large wire transfers that are immediately withdrawn by a check or debit card.
- A customer attempts to cancel a transaction after learning of currency transaction reporting, information verification, or record keeping requirements related to the transaction.

Internal Control Forms and Checklists

Figure 1 – Internal Control Assessment Form

1. Document Your Understanding of the Control Environment

In the space provided below, indicate whether you strongly agree, somewhat agree, some-what disagree, or strongly disagree with the following statements. Your answers should be based on

- ▶ Your previous experience with the entity
- ▶ Inquiries of appropriate management, supervisory, and staff personnel
- ▶ Inspection of documents and records
- ▶ Observation of the entity's activities and operations

	No Opinion	Strongly Disagree	Some what Disagree	Some what Agree	Strongly Agree
A. Control Environment Factors **Integrity and Ethical Values**					
1.. Management has high ethical and behavioral standards					
2. The company has a written code of ethical and behavioral standards that is comprehensive and periodically acknowledged by all employees.					
3. If a written code of conduct does not exist, the management culture emphasizes the importance of integrity and ethical values.					
4. Management reinforces its ethical and behavioral standards.					
5. Management appropriately deals with signs that problems exist (e.g., defective products or hazardous waste) even when the cost of identifying and solving the problem could be high.					
6. Management has removed or reduced incentives and temptations that might prompt personnel to engage in dishonest, illegal, or unethical acts. *For example, there is generally no* Pressure to meet unrealistic performance targets. High-performance-dependent rewards.					

	No Opinion	Strongly Disagree	Some what Disagree	Some what Agree	Strongly Agree
Upper and lower cutoffs on bonus plans.					
7. Management has provided guidance on the situations and frequency with which intervention of established controls is appropriate.					
8. Management intervention is documented and explained appropriately.					
Commitment to Competence					
9. Management has appropriately considered the knowledge and skill levels necessary to accomplish financial reporting tasks.					
10. Employees with financial reporting tasks generally have the knowledge and skills necessary to accomplish those tasks.					
Board of Directors and Audit Committee					
11. The board of directors is independent from management.					
12. The board constructively challenges management's planned decisions.					
13. Directors have sufficient knowledge and industry experience and time to serve effectively.					
14. The board regularly receives the information they need to monitor management's objectives and strategies.					

	No Opinion	Strongly Disagree	Some what Disagree	Some what Agree	Strongly Agree
15. The audit committee reviews the scope of activities of the internal and external auditors annually.					
16. The audit committee meets privately with the chief financial and/or accounting officers, internal auditors and external auditors to discuss the					
▶ Reasonableness of the financial reporting process					
▶ System of internal control					
▶ Significant comments and recommendations					
▶ Management's performance					
17. The board takes steps to ensure an appropriate "tone at the top."					
18. The board or committee takes action as a result of its findings.					

Management's Philosophy and Operating Style

	No Opinion	Strongly Disagree	Some what Disagree	Some what Agree	Strongly Agree
19. Management moves carefully, proceeding only after carefully analyzing the risks and potential benefits of accepting business risks.					
20. Management is generally cautious or conservative in financial reporting and tax matters.					
21. There is relatively low turnover of key personnel (e.g., operating,accounting, data processing, internal audit).					

	No Opinion	Strongly Disagree	Some what Disagree	Some what Agree	Strongly Agree
22. There is no undue pressure to meet budget, profit, or other financial and operating goals.					
23. Management views the accounting and internal audit function as a vehicle for exercising control over the entity's activities.					
24. Operating personnel review and "sign off" on reported results.					
25. Senior managers frequently visit subsidiary or divisional operations.					
26. Group or divisional management meetings are held frequently.					
Organizational Structure					
27. The entity's organizational structure facilitates the flow of information upstream, downstream, and across all business activities.					
28. Responsibilities and expectations for the entity's business activities are communicated clearly to the executives in charge of those activities.					
29. The executives in charge have the required knowledge, experience, and training to perform their duties.					
30. Those in charge of business activities have access to senior operating management.					

	No Opinion	Strongly Disagree	Some what Disagree	Some what Agree	Strongly Agree
Assignment of Authority and Responsibility					
31. Authority and responsibility are delegated only to the degree necessary to achieve the company's objectives.					
32. Job descriptions, for at least management and supervisory personnel, exist.					
33. Job descriptions contain specific references to control related responsibilities.					
34. Proper resources are provided for personnel to carry out their duties.					
35. Personnel understand the entity's objectives and know how their individual actions interrelate and contribute to those objectives.					
36. Personnel recognize how and for what they will be held accountable.					
Human Resource Policies and Practices					
37. The entity generally hires the most qualified people for the job.					
38. Hiring and recruiting practices emphasize educational background, prior work experience, past accomplishments, and evidence of integrity and ethical behavior.					
39. Recruiting practices include formal, in-depth employment interviews.					

	No Opinion	Strongly Disagree	Some what Disagree	Some what Agree	Strongly Agree
40. Prospective employees are told of the entity's history, culture and operating style.					
41. The entity provides training opportunities, and employees are well-trained.					
42. Promotions and rotation of personnel are based on periodic performance appraisals.					
43. Methods of compensation, including bonuses, are designed to motivate personnel and reinforce outstanding performance.					
44. Management does not hesitate to take disciplinary action when violations of expected behavior occur.					

B. Other Internal Control Components with a Pervasive Effect on the Organization

Risk Assessment

	No Opinion	Strongly Disagree	Some what Disagree	Some what Agree	Strongly Agree
1. Special action is taken to ensure new personnel understand their tasks.					
2. Management appropriately considers the control activities performed by personnel who change jobs or leave the company.					
3. Management assesses how new accounting and information systems will impact internal control.					

	No Opinion	Strongly Disagree	Some what Disagree	Some what Agree	Strongly Agree
4. Management reconsiders the appropriateness of existing control activities when new accounting and information systems are developed and implemented.					
5. Employees are adequately trained when accounting and information systems are changed or replaced.					
6. Accounting and information system capabilities are upgraded when the volume of information increases significantly.					
7. Accounting and data processing personnel are expanded as needed when the volume of information increases significantly.					
8. The entity has the ability to forecast reasonably operating and financial results.					
9. Management keeps abreast of the political, regulatory, business, and social culture of areas in which foreign operations exist.					
General Control Activities					
10. The entity prepares operating budgets and cash flow projections.					
11. Operating budgets and projections lend themselves to effective comparison with actual results.					

	No Opinion	Strongly Disagree	Some what Disagree	Some what Agree	Strongly Agree
12. Significant variances between budgeted or projected amounts and actual results are reviewed and explained.					
13. The company has adequate safekeeping facilities for custody of the accounting records such as fireproof storage areas and restricted access cabinets.					
14. The entity has a suitable record retention plan.					
15. The entity has adequate controls to limit access to computer programs and data files.					
16. Periodically, personnel compare counts of assets to amounts shown on control records.					
17. There is adequate segregation of duties among those responsible for authorizing transactions, recording transactions, and maintaining custody of assets.					
Information and Communication Systems Support					
18. Management receives the information they need to carry out their responsibilities.					
19. Information is provided at the right level of detail for different levels of management.					
20. Information is available on a timely basis.					

	No Opinion	Strongly Disagree	Some what Disagree	Some what Agree	Strongly Agree
21. Information with accounting significance (for example, slow-paying customers) is transmitted across functional lines in a timely manner.					
Monitoring					
22. Customer complaints about billings are investigated for their underlying causes.					
23. Communications from bankers, regulators, or other outside parties are monitored for items of accounting significance.					
24. Management responds appropriately to auditor recommendations on ways to strengthen internal controls.					
25. Employees are required to "sign off" to evidence the performance of critical control functions.					
26. The internal auditors are independent of the activities they audit.					
27. Internal auditors have adequate training and experience.					
28. Internal auditors document the planning and execution of their work by such means as audit programs and working papers.					
29. Internal audit reports are submitted to the board of directors or audit committee.					

II. Determine Other Areas for Evaluation

The completion of section I of this form is the first of several forms that may be used to document your understanding of internal controls sufficiently to plan a primarily substantive audit. In the space provided below, determine which of the following areas apply. A "Yes" answer generally indicates you should complete the related form.

	No	Yes	W/P Ref.
Significant Account Balances and Transaction Cycles			
1. The following account balances or transaction cycles are significant to the company's financial statements.			
a. Revenue Cycle, including sales, accounts receivable, or cash receipts. (Normally considered significant for most businesses.)			
If yes, the related Financial Reporting Information Systems and Controls Check-list can be found at			
b. Purchasing Cycle, including purchasing, accounts payable, or cash disbursements. (Normally considered significant for most businesses.)			
If yes, the related Financial Reporting Information Systems and Controls Check-list can be found at			
c. Inventory, including inventory and cost sales.			
If yes, the related Financial Reporting Information Systems and Controls Check-list can be found at			
d. Financing, including investments and debt.			
If yes, the related Financial Reporting Information Systems and Controls Check-list can be found at			
e. Property, Plant, and Equipment, including fixed assets and depreciation.			
If yes, the related Financial Reporting Information Systems and Controls Check-list can be found at			

	No	Yes	W/P Ref.
f. Payroll.			
If yes, the related Financial Reporting Information Systems and Controls Check-list can be found at			

III. Assess Lack of Segregation of Duties

In the space provided below, assess risk due to a lack of segregation of duties for the company, based on the completion of sections I and II of this form. Your comments should address:

▶ The person with incompatible responsibilities and the nature of those responsibilities.

▶ Any mitigating factors or controls, such as direct management oversight.

▶ The risk that material misstatements might occur as a result of a lack of segregation of duties, and the type of those misstatements.

▶ How substantive procedures will be designed to limit the risk of those misstatements to an acceptable level.

IV. Assess the Risk of Management Override

Even in effectively controlled entities—those with generally high levels of integrity and control consciousness-a manager might be able to override controls. The term management override means—

Overruling prescribed policies or procedures for illegitimate purposes with the intent of personal gain or enhanced presentation of an entity's financial condition or compliance status.

Management might override the control system for many reasons: to increase reported revenue, to boost market value of the entity prior to sale, to meet sales or earnings projections, to bolster bonus pay-outs tied to performance, to appear to cover violations of debt covenant agreements, or to hide lack of compliance with legal requirements. Override practices include deliberate misrepresentations to bankers, lawyers, accountants, and vendors, and intentionally issuing false documents such as sales invoices.

An active, involved board of directors can significantly reduce the risk of management override.

Management override is different from management intervention, which is the over-rule of prescribed policies or procedures for legitimate purposes. For example, management intervention is usually necessary to deal with nonrecurring and nonstandard transactions or events that otherwise might be handled by the system.

In the space below, assess the risk of management override for this company. You should consider the risk that management override possibilities exist, the risk that management will take advantage of those possibilities, and any evidence that management has engaged in override practices. If the risk of management override is greater than low, indicate how planned audit procedures will reduce this risk to an acceptable level.

V. Interpret Results

You should consider the collective effect of the strengths and weaknesses in various control components. Management's strengths and weaknesses may have a pervasive effect on internal control. For example, management controls may mitigate a lack of segregation of duties. However, human resource policies and practices directed toward hiring competent financial and accounting personnel may not mitigate a strong bias by management to overstate earnings.

A. Areas That May Allow for Control Risk to Be Assessed Below the Maximum

Based on the completion of sections I through IV of this form you may have become aware of certain accounts, transactions, and assertions where it may be possible and efficient to plan a control risk assessment below the maximum. In the area below, document those accounts, transactions, and assertions and the related tests of controls.

Accounts, Transactions, and Assertions	Test of Controls Working Paper Reference

B. Areas of Possible Control Weakness

Based on the completion of sections I through IV of this form, you may have become aware of certain areas that may indicate possible control weaknesses, not including those areas relating to segregation of duties and management override which were assessed and documented in sections III and IV.

In the space provided below, document those areas of possible weakness and the impact the identified weakness will have on the audit. Discuss—

▶ The nature of the identified possible weakness
▶ Any mitigating factors or controls, such as direct management oversight
▶ The risk that material misstatements might occur as a result of the weakness and the type of those misstatements
▶ How substantive procedures will be designed to reduce the risk of those misstatements to an acceptable level.

VI. Document Your Conclusion with Respect to Internal Controls

	20_	20-	20-	20-

Prepared or updated by: In-Charge
Reviewed by:

Figure 2 — Computer Applications Checklist—Medium to Large Business

.01 This questionnaire may be used to document your understanding of the way computers are used in the information and communication systems of a medium to large business.

I. Computer Hardware

Describe the computer hardware for the entity, and its configuration. Consider—

> The make and model of company's main processing computer(s)
>
> Input and output devices
>
> Storage means and capabilities
>
> Local area networks
>
> Stand-alone microcomputers

You may wish to attach a separate page to this checklist to document the entity's computer hardware.

_____

_____

_____

_____

_____

II. Computer Software

Describe the entity's main software packages and whether they are unmodified, commercially available packages, or were developed or modified in-house. (End-user computing applications will be considered only for significant account balances and transaction cycles. See the Financial Reporting Information Systems and Control Checklist— Medium to Large Business.)

	Unmodified Commercial	In-House	N/A
Operating system Access control General accounting Network Database management Communications Utilities Other:			

II. Computer Control Environment

In the space provided below, indicate whether you strongly agree, somewhat agree, some-what disagree, or strongly disagree with the following statements. Your answers should be based on—

Your previous experience with the entity

Inquiries of appropriate management, supervisory, and staff personnel

Inspection of documents and records

Observation of the entity's activities and operations

	No Opinion	Strongly Disagree	Somewhat Disagree	Somewhat Agree	Strongly Agree
Acquisition of Hardware					
1. The company has a coherent management plan for the purchase and continued investment in computer hardware.					
2. The computer hardware is sufficient to meet the company's needs.					
3. The company's computer hardware is safely and properly installed.					

	No Opinion	Strongly Disagree	Somewhat Disagree	Somewhat Agree	Strongly Agree
4. The company has standard, regular hardware maintenance procedures.					
Acquisition of Software					
5. The company has a coherent management plan for the purchase of and continued investment in computer software.					
6. The company researches software products to determine whether they meet the needs of the intended users.					
7. The company's application programs are compatible with each other.					
8. The company obtains recognized software from reputable sources.					
9. Company policy prohibits the use of unauthorized programs introduced by employees.					
10. Company policy prohibits the downloading of untested software from sources such as dial-up bulletin boards.					
11. The company uses virus protection software to screen for virus infections.					
Program Development					
12. Users are involved in the design and approval of systems.					

	No Opinion	Strongly Disagree	Somewhat Disagree	Somewhat Agree	Strongly Agree
13. Users review the completion of various phases of the application.					
14. New programs are thoroughly tested.					
15. Users are involved in the review of tests of the program.					
16. Adequate procedures exist to transfer programs from development to production libraries.					
Program Changes					
17. Users are involved in the design and approval of program changes.					
18. Program changes are thoroughly tested.					
19. Users are involved in the review of tests of the program changes.					
20. Adequate procedures exit to transfer changed programs from development to production libraries.					
Logical Access					
21. Management has identified confidential and sensitive data for which access should be restricted.					
22. Procedures are in place to restrict access to confidential and sensitive data.					

	No Opinion	Strongly Disagree	Somewhat Disagree	Somewhat Agree	Strongly Agree
23. Procedures are in place to reduce the risk of unauthorized transactions being entered into processing.					
24. The use of utility programs is controlled or monitored carefully.					
25. Procedures are in place to detect unauthorized changes to programs supporting the financial statements.					
26. Programmer access to production programs, live data files, and job control language is controlled.					
27. Operator access to source code and individual elements of data files is controlled.					
28. Users have access only to defined programs and data files.					
Physical Security					
29. The company has established procedures for the periodic back-up of files.					
30. Back-up procedures include multiple generations.					
31. Back-up files are stored in a secure, off-site location.					
Computer Operations					
32. Operations management reviews lists of regular and unscheduled batch jobs.					

	No Opinion	Strongly Disagree	Somewhat Disagree	Somewhat Agree	Strongly Agree
33. Job control instruction sets are menu-driven.					
34. Jobs are executed only from the operator's terminal.					

IV. Outside Computer Service Organizations

This section should be used to document your understanding of how the company uses an outside computer service organization to process significant accounting information. Guidance on auditing entities that use computer service organizations is contained in SAS No. 70, Reports on the Processing of Transactions by Service Organizations (AU section 324).

1. List the name of the service organization and the general types of services it provides.

2. Are the general ledger and other primary accounting records processed by an outside service organization?   Yes   No

    If yes, describe the source documents provided to the service organization, the reports and other documentation received from the organization, and the controls maintained by the user over input and output to prevent or detect material misstatement.

    _____

    _____

    _____

3. List the type and date of the most recent service auditor report.

Figure 3 — Financial Reporting Information and Controls Checklist— Medium to Large Business

Revenue Cycle

Revenue, Accounts Receivable, and Cash Receipts

.01 This checklist may be used on any audit engagement of a medium to large company when the revenue cycle is significant. Normally, the revenue cycle is significant in most audit engagements.

.02 The purpose of this checklist is to document your understanding of controls for significant classes of transactions. Your knowledge of the revenue cycle should be sufficient for you to understand—

▶ How cash and credit sales are initiated
▶ How credit limits are established and maintained
▶ How cash receipts are recorded
▶ How sales and cash receipts are processed by the accounting system
▶ The accounting records and supporting documents involved in the processing and reporting of sales, accounts receivable, and cash receipts
▶ The processes used to prepare significant accounting estimates and disclosures

Interpreting Results

.03 This checklist documents your understanding of how internal control over the revenue cycle is designed and whether it has been placed in operation. It should help you in planning a primarily substantive approach. To assess control risk below the maximum, you will need to design tests of controls and then test specific controls to determine the effectiveness of their design and operation.

.04 The processes, documents, and controls listed on this questionnaire are typical for medium to large business entities but are by no means all-inclusive. The preponderance of "No" or "N/A" responses may indicate that the entity uses other processes, documents, or controls in their information and communication systems. You should consider supplementing this questionnaire with a memo or flowchart to document significant features of the client's system that are not covered by this questionnaire. See AAM section 4500 for example flowcharting techniques.

.05			Personnel	N/A	No	Yes
1.		**Revenue and Accounts Receivable**				
A.		Initiating Sales Transactions				
	1.	Credit limits are clearly defined.				
	2.	Credit limits are clearly communicated.				
	3.	The credit of prospective customers is investigated before it is extended to them.				
	4.	Credit limits are periodically reviewed.				
	5.	The people who perform the credit function are independent of— Sales Billing Collection Accounting				
	6.	Credit limits and changes in credit limits are communicated to persons responsible for approving sales orders on a timely basis.				
	7.	The company has clearly defined policies and procedures for acceptance and approval of sales orders.				
	8.	Prenumbered sales orders are used and accounted for.				
	9.	Prenumbered shipping documents are used to record shipments.				
	10.	Shipping document information is verified prior to shipment.				

		Personnel	N/A	No	Yes
11.	The people who perform the shipping function are independent of— ▶ Sales ▶ Billing ▶ Collection ▶ Accounting				
12.	All shipping documents are accounted for.				
13.	Prenumbered credit memos are used to document sales returns.				
14.	All credit memos are approved and accounted for.				
15.	Credit memos are matched with receiving reports for returned goods.				
16.	Cash sales are controlled by cash registers or prenumbered cash receipts forms.				
17.	Someone other than the cashier has custody of the cash register tape compartment.				
18.	Someone other than the cashier takes periodic readings of the cash register and balances the cash on hand.				
B.	**Processing Sales Transactions**				
19.	Information necessary to prepare invoices (e.g., prices, discount policies) is clearly communicated to billing personnel on a timely basis.				
20.	Prenumbered invoices are prepared promptly after goods are shipped.				

		Personnel	N/A	No	Yes
21.	Quantities on the invoices are compared to shipping documents.				
22.	The prices on the invoices are current.				
23.	The people who perform the billing function are independent of— ▶ Sales ▶ Credit ▶ Collection				
24.	Invoices are mailed to customers on a timely basis.				
25.	Invoices are posted to the general ledger on a timely basis.				
26.	Standard journal entries are used to record sales.				
27.	Invoices are posted to the sales and accounts receivable subsidiary ledgers or journals on a timely basis.				
28.	Credit memos are posted to the general ledger on a timely basis.				
29.	Credit memos are posted to the sales and accounts receivable subsidiary ledgers or journals on a timely basis.				
30.	Procedures exist for determining proper cut-off of sales at month-end.				
31.	The sales and accounts receivable balances shown in the general ledger are reconciled to the sales and accounts receivable subsidiary ledgers on a regular basis.				

	Personnel	N/A	No	Yes
C. **Estimates and Disclosures for Sales Transactions**				
29. The accounting system generates a monthly aging of accounts receivable.				
30. The people who prepare the aging are independent of— Billing Collection				
34. Management uses the accounts receivable aging to investigate, write off, or adjust delinquent accounts receivable.				
35. Management uses the accounts receivable aging and other information to estimate an allowance for doubtful accounts.				
36. The person responsible for financial reporting identifies significant concentrations of credit risk.				

II. Cash Receipts

A.   Initiating Cash Receipts Transactions

	Personnel	N/A	No	Yes
1. The entity maintains records of payments on accounts by customer.				
2. Someone other than the person responsible for maintaining accounts receivable opens the mail and lists the cash receipts.				
3. Cash receipts are deposited intact.				

	Personnel	N/A	No	Yes
4. Cash receipts are deposited in separate bank accounts when required.				
5. People who handle cash receipts are adequately bonded.				
6. Local bank accounts used for branch office collections are subject to withdrawal only by the home office.				
B. Processing Cash Received on Account				
7. Cash receipts are posted to the general ledger on a timely basis.				
8 Cash receipts are posted to the accounts receivable subsidiary ledger on a timely basis.				
9. Standard journal entries are used to post cash receipts.				
10. The people who enter cash receipts to the accounting system are independent of the physical handling of collections.				
11. Timely bank reconciliations are prepared or reviewed by someone independent of the cash receipts function.				

End User Computing in the Revenue Cycle

.06   End-user computing occurs when the user is responsible for the development and execution of the computer application that generates the information used by that same person. For example, an accounting clerk prepares a spreadsheet which shows amortization of premiums or discounts, and the information from the spreadsheet is the source of a journal entry.

.07   The Computer Applications Checklist—Medium to Large Business was used to document your understanding of computer applications operated by the company's MIS department. In this section of the Financial Reporting Information Systems and Controls Checklist, you may document your understanding of how end user computing is used in the revenue cycle to process significant accounting information outside of the MIS department.

.08   You should obtain an understanding of any spreadsheet application, database, or separate computer system that has been developed by end users to—

Process significant accounting information outside of the MIS-operated accounting application. For example, a spreadsheet accumulates invoices for batch processing.

Make significant accounting decisions. For example, a spreadsheet application that ages accounts receivable and helps in determining writeoffs.

Accumulate footnote information. For example, a database of customers provides information about the location of customers for possible concentration of credit risk disclosures.

.09   In the space provided below, describe how end-user computing is used in the revenue cycle. Describe—

The person or department who performs the computing

A general description of the application and its type (e.g., spreadsheet)

The source of the information used in the application

How the results of the application are used in further processing or decision making

_____

_____

_____

_____

Procedures and Controls over End-User Computing

.10   Answer the following questions relating to procedures and controls over end user computing related to the revenue cycle.

	Personnel	N/A	No	Yes
Revenue Cycle				
1. End-user applications listed in paragraph .09 of this form have been adequately tested before use.				
2. The application has an appropriate level of built-in controls, such as edit checks, range tests, or reasonableness checks.				
3. Access controls limit access to the end-user application.				
4. A mechanism exists to prevent or detect the use of incorrect versions of data files.				
5. The output of the end user applications is reviewed for accuracy or reconciled to the source information.				

Information Processed by Outside Computer Service Organizations

11. The Computer Applications Checklist—Medium to Large Business Computer Applications was used to document your understanding of the client's use of an outside computer service organization to process entity-wide accounting information such as the general ledger. In this section you will document your understanding of how the entity uses an outside computer service organization to process information relating specifically to the revenue cycle.

12. In the space below, describe the revenue cycle information processed by the out-side computer service bureau. Discuss—
   ▶ The general nature of the application
   ▶ The source documents used by the service organization
   ▶ The reports or other accounting documents produced by the service organization

▶ The nature of the service organization's responsibilities. Do they merely record entity transactions and process related data, or do they have the ability to initiate transactions on their own?

▶ Controls maintained by the entity to prevent or detect material misstatement in the input or output.

_____

_____

_____

_____

_____

_____

Purchasing Cycle

Purchasing, Accounts Payable, and Cash Disbursements

13. This checklist may be used on any audit engagement of a medium to large business where the purchasing cycle is significant. Normally, the purchasing cycle is significant for most businesses.

14. The purpose of this checklist is to document your understanding of controls for significant classes of transactions. Your knowledge of the purchasing cycle should be sufficient for you to understand—

▶ How purchases are initiated and goods received

▶ How cash disbursements are recorded

▶ How purchases and cash disbursements are processed by the financial reporting information system

▶ The accounting records and supporting documents involved in the processing and reporting of purchases, accounts payable, and cash disbursements

▶ The processes used to prepare significant accounting estimates and disclosures

Interpreting Results

15. This checklist documents your understanding of how internal control over the purchasing cycle is designed and whether it has been placed in operation. It should help you in planning a primarily substantive approach. To assess control risk below the maxi-mum, you will need to design tests of controls and then test specific controls to determine the effectiveness of their design and operation.

16. The processes, documents, and controls listed on this questionnaire are typical for medium to large business entities but are by no

means all-inclusive. The preponderance of "No" or "N/A" responses may indicate that the entity uses other processes, documents, or controls in their information and communication systems. You should consider supplementing this questionnaire with a memo or flowchart to document significant features of the client's system that are not covered by this questionnaire. See AAM section 4500 for example flowcharting techniques.

17.

	Personnel	N/A	No	Yes
1. Purchases and Accounts Payable				
A. Initiating Purchases and Receipt of Goods				
1. All purchases over a predetermined amount are approved by management.				
2. Nonroutine purchases (for example, services, fixed assets, or investments) are approved by management.				
3. A purchase order system is used, prenumbered purchase orders are accounted for, and physical access to purchase orders is controlled.				
4. Open purchase orders are periodically reviewed,				
5. The purchasing function is independent o f — ReceivingInvoice processingCash disbursements				
6. All goods are inspected and counted when received.				
7. Prenumbered receiving reports, or a log, are used to record the receipt of goods.				
8. The receiving reports or log indicate the date the items were received.				
9. The receiving function is independent o f — Purchasing Invoice processingCash disbursements				
B. **Processing Purchases**				
10. Invoices from vendors are matched with applicable receiving reports.				

	Personnel	N/A	No	Yes
11. Invoices are reviewed for proper quantity and prices, and mathematical accuracy.				
12. Invoices from vendors are posted to the general ledger on a timely basis.				
13. Invoices from vendors are posted to the accounts payable subsidiary ledger on a timely basis.				
14. The invoice processing function is independent o f — ▶ Purchasing ▶ Receiving ▶ Cash disbursements				
15. Standard journal entries are used to post accounts payable.				
16. Accounts payable account per the general ledger is reconciled periodically to the accounts payable subsidiary ledger.				
17. Statements from vendors are reconciled to the accounts payable subsidiary ledger.				
C. Disclosures				
18. Management has the information to identify vulnerability due to concentrations of suppliers (SOP 94-6).				
II. Cash Disbursements				
A. Initiating Cash Disbursements				
1. All disbursements except those from petty cash are made by check.				
2. All checks are recorded.				
3. Supporting documentation such as invoices and receiving reports are reviewed before the checks are signed.				
4. Supporting documents are canceled to avoid duplicate payment.				

	Personnel	N/A	No	Yes
B. **Processing Cash Disbursements**				
5. Cash disbursements are posted to the general ledger on a timely basis.				
6. Cash disbursements are posted to the accounts payable subsidiary ledger on a timely basis.				
7. Standard journal entries are used to post cash disbursements.				
8. Timely bank reconciliations are prepared or reviewed by the owner or manager or someone independent of the cash receipts function.				

End-User Computing in the Purchasing Cycle

18 End-user computing occurs when the user is responsible for the development and execution of the computer application that generates the information used by that same person. For example, an accounting clerk prepares a spreadsheet that amortizes premiums or discounts, and the information from the spreadsheet is the source of a journal entry.

19 The Computer Applications Checklist—Medium to Large Business was used to document your understanding of computer applications operated by the company's MIS department. In this section of the Financial Reporting Information Systems and Controls Checklist, you may document your understanding of how end-user computing is used in the purchasing cycle to process significant accounting information outside of the MIS department.

20 You should obtain an understanding of any spreadsheet application, database, or separate computer system that has been developed by end-users t o —
  ▸ Process significant accounting information outside of the MIS-operated accounting application. For example, a spreadsheet accumulates nonroutine purchases for batch processing
  ▸ Make significant accounting decisions
  ▸ Accumulate footnote information. For example, a database of vendors provides information for possible concentration of risk disclosures

21 In the space provided below, describe how end user computing is used in the purchasing cycle. Describe—
  ▸ The person or department who performs the computing
  ▸ A general description of the application and its type (e.g., spreadsheet)

▶ The source of the information used in the application

▶ How the results of the application are used in further processing or decision making

Procedures and Controls Over End User Computing

22 Answer the following questions relating to procedures and controls over end user computing related to the purchasing cycle.

	Personnel	N/A	No	Yes
Purchasing Cycle				
1. End user applications listed in paragraph .21 of this form have been adequately tested before use.				
2. The application has an appropriate level of built-in controls, such as edit checks, range tests, or reasonableness checks.				
3. Access controls limit access to the end user application.				
4. A mechanism exists to prevent or detect the use of incorrect versions of data files.				
5. The output of the end-user applications is reviewed for accuracy or reconciled to the source information.				

Information Processed by Outside Computer Service Organizations

23 The Computer Applications Checklist—Medium to Large Business was used to document your understanding of the client's use of an outside computer service organization to process entity-wide accounting information such as

the general ledger. In this section you will document your understanding of how the entity uses an outside computer service organization to process information relating specifically to the purchasing cycle.

.24 In the space below, describe the purchasing cycle information processed by the outside computer service bureau. Discuss—

▶ The general nature of the application.

▶ The source documents used by the service organization.

▶ The reports or other accounting documents produced by the service organization.

▶ The nature of the service organization's responsibilities. Do they merely record entity transactions and process related data, or do they have the ability to initiate transactions on their own?

▶ Controls maintained by the entity to prevent or detect material misstatement in the input or output.

Inventory

Inventory and Cost of Sales

.25 This checklist may be used on any audit engagement of a medium to large business where inventory is a significant transaction cycle.

.26 The purpose of this checklist is to document your understanding of controls for significant classes of transactions. Your knowledge of the inventory cycle should be sufficient for you to understand—

▶ How costs are capitalized to inventory

▶ How cost is relieved from inventory

▶ How inventory costs and cost of sales are processed by the accounting system

▶ The procedures used to take the physical inventory count

▶ The accounting records and supporting documents involved in the processing and reporting of inventory and cost of sales

▶ The processes used to prepare significant accounting estimates and disclosures

Interpreting Results

.27 This checklist documents your understanding of how internal control over the inventory cycle is designed and whether it has been placed in operation. It should help you in planning a primarily substantive approach. To assess control risk below the maximum, you will need to design tests of controls and then test specific controls to determine the effectiveness of their design and operation.

.28 The processes, documents, and controls listed on this questionnaire are typical for medium to large business entities but are by no means all-inclusive. The preponderance of "No" or "N/A" responses may indicate that the entity uses other processes, documents, or controls in their information and communication systems. You should consider supplementing this questionnaire with a memo or flowchart to document significant features of the client's system that are not covered by this questionnaire. See AAM section 4500 for example flowcharting techniques.

.29

	Personnel	N/A	No	Yes
1. Inventory and Cost of Sales				
A. Capturing Capitalizable Costs[1]				
1. Management prepares production goals and schedules based on sales forecasts.				
2. The company budgets its planned inventory levels.				
You should also consider completing the Financial Reporting Information Systems and Controls Checklist for the purchasing cycle to document your understanding of how the purchase of inventory is initiated.				
3. All releases from storage of raw materials, supplies, and purchased parts inventory are based on approved requisition documents.				
4. Labor costs are reported promptly and in sufficient detail to allow for the proper allocation to inventory.				
5. The entity uses a cost accounting system to accumulate capitalizable costs.				
6. The cost accounting system distinguishes between costs that should be capitalized for GAAP purposes and those that should be capitalizable for tax purposes.				

		Personnel	N/A	No	Yes
7.	For standard cost systems:				
a	Standard rates and volume are periodically compared to actual and revised accordingly.				
b	Significant variances are investigated.				
8.	The cost accounting system interfaces with the general ledger.				
9.	Transfers of completed units from production to custody of finished goods inventory are based on approved completion reports that authorize the transfer.				
10.	The people responsible for maintaining detailed inventory records are independent from the physical custody and handling of inventories.				
11.	Production cost budgets are periodically compared to actual costs, and significant differences are explained.				
B. Inventory Records					
12.	The entity maintains adequate inventory records of prices and amounts on hand.				
13.	Withdrawals from inventory are based on prenumbered finished inventory requisitions, shipping reports, or both.				
14.	Additions to and withdrawals from inventory are posted to the inventory records and the general ledger.				
15.	Standard journal entries are used to post inventory transactions to the inventory records and the general ledger.				
16.	Inventory records are periodically reconciled to the general ledger.				

		Personnel	N/A	No	Yes
	17. Inventory records are reconciled to a physical inventory count.				
C.	**Physical Inventory Counts**				
	18. Inventory is counted at least once a year				
	19. Physical inventory counters are giver adequate instructions.				
	20. Inventory count procedures are sufficient to provide an accurate count, including steps to ensure—Proper cut-off Identification of obsolete items All items are counted once and only once				
D.	**Estimates and Disclosures**				
	21. Management is able to identify excess, slow-moving, or obsolete inventory.				
	22. Excess, slow-moving, or obsolete inventory is periodically written off.				
	23. Management can identify inventory subject to rapid technological obsolescence that may need to be disclosed under SOP 94-6.				

End-User Computing in the Inventory Cycle

.30 End-user computing occurs when the user is responsible for the development and execution of the computer application that generates the information used by that same person. For example, an accounting clerk prepares a spreadsheet that amortizes premiums or discounts, and the information from the spreadsheet is the source of a journal entry.

.31 The Computer Applications Checklist—Medium to Large Business was used to document your understanding of computer applications operated by the company's MIS department. In this section of the Financial Reporting Information Systems and Controls Checklist, you may document your understanding of how end-user computing is used in the inventory cycle to process significant accounting information outside of the MIS department.

.32 You should obtain an understanding of any spreadsheet application, database, or separate computer system that has been developed by end-users t o —
- ▶ Process significant accounting information outside the MIS-operated accounting application. For example, a spreadsheet calculates overhead cost allocations.
- ▶ Make significant accounting decisions. A spreadsheet application tracks slow-moving items for possible write-off.
- ▶ Accumulate footnote information.

.33 In the space provided below, describe how end user computing is used in the inventory cycle. Describe—
- ▶ The person or department who performs the computing.
- ▶ A general description of the application and its type (e.g., spreadsheet).
- ▶ The source of the information used in the application.
- ▶ How the results of the application are used in further processing or decision making.

Procedures and Controls Over End-User Computing

.34 Answer the following questions relating to procedures and controls over end user computing related to the inventory cycle.

	Personnel	N/A	No	Yes
Inventory Cycle				
1. End-user applications listed i n paragraph .33 of this form have been adequately tested before use.				
2. The application has an appropriate level of built-in controls, such as edit checks, range rests, or reasonableness checks.				
3. Access controls limit access to the end user application.				
4. A mechanism exists to prevent or detect the use of incorrect versions of data files.				
5. The output of the end-user applications is reviewed for accuracy or reconciled to the source information.				

Information Processed by Outside Computer Service Organizations

.35 The Computer Applications Checklist—Medium to Large Business was used to document your understanding of the client's use of an outside computer service organization to process entity-wide accounting information such as the general ledger. In this section you will document your understanding of how the entity uses an outside computer service organization to process information relating specifically to the inventory cycle.

.36 In the space below, describe the inventory cycle information processed by the outside computer service bureau. Discuss—

  ▶ The general nature of the application.
  ▶ The source documents used by the service organization.
  ▶ The reports or other accounting documents produced by the service organization.
  ▶ The nature of the service organization's responsibilities. Do they merely record entity transactions and process related data, or do they have the ability to initiate transactions on their own?
  ▶ Controls maintained by the entity to prevent or detect material misstatement in the input or output.

Financing

Investments and Debt

.37 This checklist may be used on any audit engagement of a medium to large business where investments or debt are a significant transaction cycle.

.38 The purpose of this checklist is to document your understanding of controls for significant classes of transactions. Your knowledge of the financing cycle should be sufficient for you to understand

  ▶ How investment decisions are authorized and initiated
  ▶ How financing is authorized and captured by the accounting system
  ▶ How management classifies investments as either trading, available-for-sale, or held to maturity
  ▶ How investment and debt transactions are processed by the accounting system
  ▶ The accounting records and supporting documents involved in the processing and reporting of investments and debt
  ▶ The processes used to prepare significant accounting estimates, disclosures, and presentation

Interpreting Results

.39 This checklist documents your understanding of how internal control is designed and whether it has been placed in operation. It should help you in planning a primarily substantive approach. To assess control risk below the maximum, you will need to design tests of controls and then test specific controls to determine the effectiveness of their design and operation.

.40 The processes, documents, and controls listed on this questionnaire are typical for medium to large business entities but are by no means all-inclusive. The preponderance of "No" or "N/A" responses may indicate that the entity uses other processes, documents, or controls in their information and communication systems. You should consider supplementing this questionnaire with a memo or flowchart to document significant features of the client's system that are not covered by this questionnaire. See AAM section 4500 for example flowcharting techniques.

.41

	Personnel	N/A	No	Yes
I. Investments				
A. Authorization and Initiation				
1. Investment transactions are authorized by management.				
2. The company has established policies and procedures for determining when board of director approval is required for investment transactions.				
3. Management and the board assess and understand the risks associated with the entity's investment strategies.				
4. Investments are registered in the name of the company.				
5. At acquisition, investments are classified as trading, available-for-sale, or held-to-maturity.				

	Personnel	N/A	No	Yes
B. **Processing**				
6. Investment transactions are posted to the general ledger on a timely basis.				
7. Account statements received from brokers are reviewed for accuracy.				
8. Discounts and premiums are amortized regularly using the interest method.				
9. Procedures exist to determine the fair value of trading and available for-sale securities.				
10. The general ledger is periodically reconciled to account statements from brokers or physical counts of securities on hand.				
C. **Disclosures**				
11. Management identifies investments with off-balance-sheet credit risk for proper disclosure.				
12. Management distinguishes between derivatives held or issued for trading purposes and those held or issued for purposes other than trading.				
13. The entity accumulates the information necessary to make disclosures about derivatives.				

		Personnel	N/A	No	Yes
II.	**Debt**				
A.	**Authorization and Initiation**				
	1. Financing transactions are authorized by management.				
	2. The company has established policies and procedures for determining when board of director approval is required for financing transactions.				
	3. Management and the board assess and understand all terms, covenants, and restrictions of debt transactions.				
B.	**Processing and Documentation**				
	4. Debt transactions are posted to the general ledger on a timely basis.				
	5. Any premiums or discount are amortized using the interest method.				
	6. The company maintains Up-to-date files of all notes payable.				
C.	**Disclosure**				
	7. Procedures exist to determine the fair value of notes payable for proper disclosure.				
	8. Management reviews their compliance with debt covenants on a timely basis.				

End-User Computing in the Financing Cycle

.42 End-user computing occurs when the user is responsible for the development and execution of the computer application that generates the information used by that same person. For example, an accounting clerk prepares a spreadsheet that amortizes premiums or discounts, and the information from the spreadsheet is the source of a journal entry.

.43 The Computer Applications Checklist—Medium to Large Business was used to document your understanding of computer applications operated by the company's MIS department. In this section of the Financial Reporting Information Systems and Controls Checklist, you may document your understanding of how end-user computing is used in the financing cycle to process significant accounting information outside of the MIS department.

.44 You should obtain an understanding of any spreadsheet application, database, or separate computer system that has been developed by end-users t o —

▶ Process significant accounting information outside of the MIS-operated accounting application. For example, a spreadsheet application calculates the amortization of premiums and discounts on investments.

▶ Make significant accounting decisions.

▶ Accumulate footnote information. For example, a spreadsheet application calculates five-year debt maturities for footnote disclosure.

.45 I n the space provided below, describe how end-user computing is used in the financing cycle. Describe—

▶ The person or department who performs the computing.

▶ A general description of the application and its type (e.g., spreadsheet).

▶ The source of the information used in the application.

▶ How the results of the application are used in further processing or decision making.

_____

_____

_____

_____

_____

_____

_____

_____

_____

Procedures and Controls over End-User Computing

.46 Answer the following questions relating to procedures and controls over end user computing related to the financing cycle.

	Personnel	N/A	No	Yes
Financing Cycle				
4. End-user applications listed i n paragraph .45 of this form have been adequately tested before use.				
5. The application has an appropriate level of built-in controls, such as edit checks, range tests, or reasonableness checks.				

	Personnel	N/A	No	Yes
6. Access controls limit access to the end user application.				
7. A mechanism exists to prevent or detect the use of incorrect versions of data files.				
8. The output of the end-user applications is reviewed for accuracy or reconciled to the source information.				

Information Processed by Outside Computer Service Organizations

.47 The Computer Applications Checklist—Medium to Large Business was used to document your understanding of the client's use of an outside computer service organization to process entity-wide accounting information such as the general ledger. In this section you will document your understanding of how the entity uses an outside computer service organization to process information relating specifically to the financing cycle.

.48 In the space below, describe the financing cycle information processed by the outside computer service bureau. Discuss
  ▸ The general nature of the application.
  ▸ The source documents used by the service organization.
  ▸ The reports or other accounting documents produced by the service organization.
  ▸ The nature of the service organization's responsibilities. Do they merely record entity transactions and process related data, or do they have the ability to initiate transactions on their own?
  ▸ Controls maintained by the entity to prevent or detect material misstatement in the input or output.

Property, Plant, and Equipment

Fixed Assets and Depreciation

.49 This checklist may be used on any audit engagement where fixed assets are a significant transaction cycle.

.50 The purpose of this checklist is to document your understanding of controls for significant classes of transactions. Your knowledge of the property, plant, and equipment cycle should be sufficient for you to understand—
  ▸ How fixed asset transactions are authorized and initiated. (Additional information on the acquisition of fixed assets is documented on the Accounting Systems and Control Checklist for the Purchasing Cycle.)

▶ How fixed assets transactions and depreciation are processed by the accounting system.

▶ The accounting records and supporting documents involved in the processing and reporting of fixed assets and depreciation.

▶ The processes used to prepare significant accounting estimates and disclosures. Interpreting Results

.51 This checklist documents your understanding of how internal control over property, plant, and equipment is designed and whether it has been placed in operation. It should help you in planning a primarily substantive approach. To assess control risk below the maximum, you will need to design tests of controls and then test specific controls to determine the effectiveness of their design and operation.

.52 The processes, documents, and controls listed on this questionnaire are typical for medium to large business entities but are by no means all-inclusive. The preponderance of "No" or "N/A" responses may indicate that the entity uses other processes, documents, or controls in their information and communication systems. You should consider supplementing this questionnaire with a memo or flowchart to document significant features of the client's system that are not covered by this questionnaire. See AAM section 4500 for example flowcharting techniques.

.53

	Personnel	N/A	No	Yes
1. **Fixed Assets and Depreciation**				
A. **Authorization and Initiation**				
1. Fixed asset acquisitions and retirements are authorized by management.				
B. **Processing and Documentation**				
2. The company maintains detailed records of fixed assets and the related accumulated depreciation.				
3. Responsibilities for maintaining the fixed asset records are segregated from the custody of the assets.				
4. The general ledger and detailed fixed asset records are updated for fixed asset transactions on a timely basis.				

	Personnel	N/A	No	Yes
5. A process exists for the timely calculation of depreciation expense for both book and tax purposes.				
6. The general ledger and detailed fixed asset records are updated for depreciation expense on a timely basis.				
7. The general ledger is periodically reconciled to the detailed fixed asset records.				
C. Disclosure and Estimation				
8. Management identifies events or changes in circumstances that may indicate fixed assets have been impaired (SFAS 121).				
9. Management assesses and understands the risk of specialized equipment becoming subject to technological obsolescence (SOP 94-6).				

End-User Computing in the Property, Plant, and Equipment Cycle

.54 End-user computing occurs when the user is responsible for the development and execution of the computer application that generates the information used by that same person. For example, an accounting clerk prepares a spreadsheet that amortizes premiums or discounts, and the information from the spreadsheet is the source of a journal entry.

.55 The Computer Applications Checklist—Medium or Large Business was used to document your understanding of computer applications operated by the company's MIS department. In this section of the Financial Reporting Information Systems and Controls Checklist, you may document your understanding of how end-user computing is used in the revenue cycle to process significant accounting information outside of the MIS department.

.56 You should obtain an understanding of any spreadsheet application, database, or separate computer system that has been developed by end-users to —

> ▶ Process significant accounting information outside of the MIS-operated accounting application. For example, a spreadsheet application calculates the depreciation expense.
> ▶ Make significant accounting decisions. For example, a spreadsheet application is used to analyze lease or buy decisions.
> ▶ Accumulate footnote information.

.57 In the space provided below, describe how end-user computing is used in the property, plant, and equipment cycle. Describe—

> ▶ The person or department who performs the computing.
> ▶ A general description of the application and its type (e.g., spreadsheet).
> ▶ The source of the information used in the application.
> ▶ How the results of the application are used in further processing or decision making.

Procedures and Controls Over End-User Computing

.58 Answer the following questions relating to procedures and controls over end user computing related to the property, plant, and equipment cycle.

	Personnel	N/A	No	Yes
Property, Plant, and Equipment Cycle				
1. End user applications listed in paragraph .57 of this form have been adequately tested before use.				
2. The application has an appropriate level of built-in controls, such as edit checks, range tests, or reasonableness checks.				
3. Access controls limit access to the end-user application.				
4. A mechanism exists to pre-vent or detect the use of incorrect versions of data files.				
5. The output of the end-user applications is reviewed for accuracy or reconciled to the source information.				

Information Processed by Outside Computer Service Organizations

.59 The Computer Applications Checklist—Medium to Large Business was used to document your understanding of the client's use of an outside computer service organization to process entity-wide accounting information such as the general ledger. In this section you will document your understanding of how the entity uses an outside computer service organization to process information relating specifically to the property, plant, and equipment cycle.

.60 In the space below, describe the property, plant, and equipment cycle information processed by the outside computer service bureau. Discuss

   ▶ The general nature of the application.

   ▶ The source documents used by the service organization.

   ▶ The reports or other accounting documents produced by the service organization.

   ▶ The nature of the service organization's responsibilities. Do they merely record entity transactions and process related data, or do they have the ability to initiate transactions on their own?

   ▶ Controls maintained by the entity to prevent or detect material misstatement in the input or output.

Payroll Cycle

I. Payroll Expense

.61 This checklist may be used on any audit engagement of a medium to large business where the payroll cycle is significant.

.62 The purpose of this checklist is to document your understanding of controls for significant classes of transactions. Your knowledge of the payroll cycle should be sufficient for you to understand—

   ▶ How the time worked by employees is captured by the accounting system.

   ▶ How salaries and hourly rates are established.

   ▶ How payroll and the related withholdings are calculated.

   ▶ The accounting records and supporting documents involved in the processing and reporting of payroll.

Interpreting Results

.63 This checklist documents your understanding of how internal control over the payroll cycle is designed and whether it has been placed in operation. It should help you in planning a primarily substantive approach. To assess control risk below the maximum, you will need to design tests of controls and then test specific controls to determine the effectiveness of their design and operation.

.64 The processes, documents, and controls listed on this questionnaire are typical for medium to large business entities but are by no means all-inclusive. The preponderance of "No" or "N/A" responses may indicate that the entity uses other processes, documents, or controls in their information and communication systems. You should consider supplementing this questionnaire with a memo or flowchart to document significant features of the client's system that are not covered by this questionnaire. See AAM section 4500 for example flowcharting techniques.

.65

		Personnel	N/A	No	Yes
I.	**Payroll**				
A.	Initiating Payroll Transactions				
	1. Wages and salaries are approved by management.				
	2. Salaries of senior management are based on written authorization of the board of directors.				
	3. Bonuses are authorized by the board of directors.				
	4. Employee benefits and perks are granted in accordance with management's authorization.				
	5. Senior management benefits and perks are authorized by the board of directors.				
	6. Proper authorization is obtained for all payroll deductions..				
	7. Access to personnel files is limited to those who are independent of the payroll or cash functions.				
	8. Wage and salary rates and payroll deductions are reported promptly to employees who perform the pay-roll processing function.				
	9. Changes in wage and salary rates and payroll deductions are reported promptly to employees who perform the payroll processing function.				

			Personnel	N/A	No	Yes
	10.	Adequate time records are maintained for employees paid by the hour.				
	11.	Time records for hourly employees are approved by a supervisor.				
B.	**Processing Payroll**					
	12.	Payroll is calculated using authorized pay rates, payroll deductions, and time records.				
	13	Payroll registers are reviewed for accuracy.				
	14.	Standard journal entries are used to post payroll transactions to the general ledger.				
	15.	Payroll cost distributions are reconciled to gross pay.				
	16.	Payroll information such as hours worked is periodically compared to production records.				
	17.	Net pay is distributed by persons who are independent of personnel, payroll preparation, time-keeping, and check preparation functions.				
	18.	The responsibility for custody and follow-up of unclaimed wages is assigned to someone who is independent of personnel, payroll processing, and cash disbursement functions.				
	19.	Procedures are in place to estimate the fair value of stock-based compensation plans.				

End-User Computing in the Payroll Cycle

.66 End-user computing occurs when the user is responsible for the development and execution of the computer application that generates the information used by that same person. For example, an accounting clerk prepares a spreadsheet that amortizes premiums or discounts, and the information from the spreadsheet is the source of a journal entry.

.67 The Computer Applications Checklist—Medium to Large Business was used to document your understanding of off-the-shelf computer software accounting applications such as the general ledger. In this section of the Financial Reporting Information Systems and Controls Checklist, you may document your understanding of how end-user computing is used in the payroll cycle to process significant accounting information outside of the general accounting software.

.68 You should obtain an understanding of any spreadsheet application, database, or separate computer system that has been developed by end-users t o —

▶ Process significant accounting information outside of the MIS-operated accounting application, for example, a spreadsheet accumulates time card information for batch processing

▶ Make significant accounting decisions, for example, a spreadsheet application is used to accumulate payroll information by job for further analysis

▶ Accumulate footnote information

.69 In the space provided below, describe how end-user computing is used in the payroll cycle. Describe—

▶ The person or department who performs the computing

▶ A general description of the application and its type (e.g., spreadsheet)

▶ The source of the information used in the application

▶ How the results of the application are used in further processing or decision making

_____

_____

_____

_____

_____

_____

Procedures and Controls Over End-User Computing

.70 Answer the following questions relating to procedures and controls over end-user computing related to the payroll cycle.

	Personnel	N/A	No	Yes
Payroll Cycle				
1. End-user applications listed in paragraph .69 of this form have been adequately tested before use.				
2. The application has an appropriate level of built-in controls, such as edit checks, range rests, or reasonableness checks.				
3. Access controls limit access to the end-user application.				
4. A mechanism exists to prevent or detect the use of incorrect versions of data files.				
5. The output of the end-user applications is reviewed for accuracy or reconciled to the source information.				

Information Processed by Outside Computer Service Organizations

.71 The Computer Applications Checklist—Medium to Large Business was used to document your understanding of the client's use of an outside computer service organization to process entity-wide accounting information such as the general ledger. In this section you will document your understanding of how the entity uses an outside computer service organization to process information relating specifically to the payroll cycle.

.72 In the space below, describe the inventory cycle information processed by the outside computer service bureau. Discuss—
- ▶ The general nature of the application.
- ▶ The source documents used by the service organization.
- ▶ The reports or other accounting documents produced by the service organization.
- ▶ The nature of the service organization's responsibilities. Do they merely record entity transactions and process related data, or do they have the ability to initiate transactions on their own?
- ▶ Controls maintained by the entity to prevent or detect material misstatement in the input or output.

Glossary

Auditing A systematic process of objectively obtaining and evaluating evidence regarding assertions about economic actions and events to ascertain the degree of correspondence between those assertions and established criteria and communicating the results to interested users

Certified Insolvency and Reorganization Accountant (CIRA) The second certification which is available to the forensic accountant. The areas of concentration are: financial reporting and taxes; managing turnaround and bankruptcy cases; and plan development and accounting.

Certified Internal Auditor (CIA) A certification, created in 1974 by the Institute of Internal auditors (IIA) (www.theiia.org). The CIA exam covers the four areas: internal audit process, internal audit skills, management control and information technology, and the audit environment.

Data mining A tool under which the data in a data warehouse are processed to identify key factors and trends in historical patterns of business activity.

Error Refers to unintentional misstatements or omissions of financial statement amounts or disclosures—for example, misinterpretation, mistakes, and use of incorrect accounting estimates. Fraud, on the other hand, refers to acts that are intentional.

External audit An audit performed by an auditor engaged in public practice leading to the expression of a professional opinion which lends credibility to the assertion under examination.

Forensic accounting A science (i.e., a department of systemized knowledge) dealing with the application of accounting facts gathered through auditing methods and procedures to resolve legal problems.

Forensic accountant An integral part of the legal team, helping to substantiate allegations, analyze facts, dispute claims, and develop motives.

Forensic Audit An examination of evidence regarding an assertion to determine its correspondence to established criteria carried out in a manner suitable to the court. An example would be a forensic audit of sales records to determine the quantum of rent owing under a lease agreement, which is the subject of litigation.

Forensic Investigation   The utilization of specialized investigative skills in carrying out an inquiry conducted in such a manner that the outcome will have application to a court of law. A forensic investigation may be grounded in accounting, medicine, engineering or some other discipline.

Fraud   In contrast to error, an illegal act (a crime) committed intentionally.

Internal audit   An audit performed by an employee who examines operational evidence to determine whether prescribed operating procedures have been followed.

Public Company Accounting Oversight Board (PCAOB) (www.pcaobus. com)   Established in 2002 as a result of the Sarbanes-Oxley Act, a private sector, non-profit corporation set up to oversee the audits of public companies and ensure that accountancy firms should no longer derive non-audit revenue streams, such as consultancy, from their audit clients.

Sarbanes-Oxley (SOX) Act   Wide-ranging U.S. corporate reform legislation, coauthored by the Democrat in charge of the Senate Banking Committee, Paul Sarbanes, and Republican Congressman Michael Oxley. It is legislation to ensure internal controls or rules to govern the creation and documentation of corporate information in financial statements. It establishes new standards for corporate accountability and penalties for corporate wrongdoing.

SAS 99   The new standard SAS No. 99 that addresses auditors' concerns regarding fulfilling their responsibility to determine if a client's financial statements are free of material misstatement due to fraud. It also illustrates how professional skepticism should be evident in all aspects of the audit; explains standard procedures that should be used to evaluate if fraud exists in a client-specific engagement; clarifies the nature of the relationship between auditors and management; and emphasizes the importance of the auditor's professional judgment.

The Association of Certified Fraud Examiners (CFEs)   Established in 1988, the 25,000-member professional organization dedicated to educating qualified individuals (Certified Fraud Examiners), who are trained in the highly specialized aspects of detecting, investigating, and deterring fraud and white-collar crime. Each member of the Association designated a Certified Fraud Examiner (CFE) has earned certification after an extensive application process and upon passing the uniform CFE Examination.

Index

A
Accounts payable 41
Attribute sampling 71
Auditing and forensic accounting 90
Auditing Standard No. 5 41
Audit program 28
    accounts payable (sample) 47
    cash in bank (sample) 37
    expense items 34
    fixed assets (sample) 39
    inventory (sample) 46
    Prepaid expenses and deferred charges
        (sample) 43
    sales and other types of income 31

C
Cash in bank 28
Certifications 123
    Certified Fraud Examiners 123
    Certified Insolvency and Reorganization
        Accountant (CIRA) 125
Certified Fraud Examiners 123
Certified Insolvency and Reorganization
    Accountant (CIRA) 125
Certified Internal Auditor (CIA) 2
Code of Ethics of The Institute of Internal
    Auditors 10
Codes of conduct 14
Compliance auditing 12
Computer Applications Checklist 147

D
Databases 64
Data mining 63, 104
Deferred charges 39

Discovery sampling 73
Divorce business valuations 99

E
Employee behavior 127
    potential signs of fraud 127
Expense items 98

F
Financial auditing 12
Financial crime indicators 127
Financial Reporting Information and Controls
    Checklist 153
Financial statement accounts
    internal audit 37
Fixed assets 18
Forensic accountant
    Divorce business valuations 101
    expert witness engagements 59
    lost earnings engagements 96
    methods of working 96
    using for
        investigations 105
        litigation support 92
Forensic accounting 94
    cases 103
    fraud examination 62
    need for 61
Forensic computing 63
Fraud
    indicators 63
    techniques for prevention 65
        awareness of risks 60
        codes of conduct 60
        controls implementation 63
        data mining 62

fraud response plan 65
On-going process 79
Recruitment 81

H
Historical reporting 21

I
Internal audit
  financial statement accounts 25
Internal audit function 15
  function 2
Internal auditing
  aspects 7
  compliance auditing 8
  comprehending 12
  evaluation 11
  financial 11
  functional 11
  management 5
  operational 6
  population 10
  preaudit 8
  program 6
  reports 6
  sample 5
  scope 7
  standards 1
  verification 14
Internal control 12
  activities 12
  appraising 15
  control environment 16
  cycle approach 16
  forms and checklists 133
    Computer Applications Checklist 147
    Financial Reporting Information and
      Controls Checklist 153
    Internal Control Assessment Form 133
  identifying deficiencies 15
  identifying fraud 15
  information and communication systems
    support 13
  Monitoring 15
  risk assessment 34
Internal Control Assessment Form 133

J
Judgement (nonstatistical) sampling 77

L
Litigation support consulting 97
Lost earnings engagements 100

M
Management auditing 11
Money laundering indicators 129

N
New reporting 21
Notes receivable 31

O
Operational auditing 11
Organizational behavior, fraud indicators 128
Overworking 127

P
Police contact 66
Prepaid expenses 39

R
Random sample, methods of choosing 69
Reporting, new 13

S
Sales 46
Sampling
  attribute 71
  discovery 73
  judgement (nonstatistical) 77
  multistage 74
  risk 68
  statistical 67
  stratified 77
  technique 70
  variables 76
Sampling risk 68
Sarbanes-Oxley Act 49
SAS 55 67
SAS 99—Consideration of Fraud in a Financial
  Statement Audit 22
Section 404 reporting 43
Securities and Exchange Commission 102
Standards for the Professional Practice of
  Internal Auditing 67

Statistical sampling 71
    attribute sampling 73
    discovery sampling 69
    methods of choosing random sample 74
    multistage sampling 68
    sampling risk 77
    stratified sampling 70
    systematic sampling technique 76
Stockholders' equity 77

T
Terrorist financing indicators 129
Tests of controls 67
    definition 67
    statistical sampling 31

V
Variables sampling 76

W
Whistleblowing policy 62